Calculations In Chem
Stoichiometry Volu

This Book Belongs To

1 In a receptacle we have 55 g of ethene that react with an excess of oxygen according the following equation:

$$C_2H_4 + O_2 \rightarrow CO_2 + H_2O \quad \text{(unbalanced)}$$

Determine:

    a) The volume obtained of carbon dioxide gas at a temperature of 0 °C and a pressure of 1 atm.

    b) Mass of water obtained.

2 We want obtain 124.2 g of water. For that, we react carbon dioxide with a percent purity of 75 % with an excess of hydrogen according the following equation:

$$CO_2 + H_2 \rightarrow CO + H_2O$$

Find:

    a) How many moles of carbon dioxide are required?

    b) How many moles of carbon monoxide are formed?

3 We want obtain 204 g of ammonia. For that, we react nitrogen with a percent purity of 57 % with an excess of hydrogen according the following equation:

$$N_2 + H_2 \rightarrow NH_3 \quad \text{(not balanced)}$$

Find:

    a) How many moles of nitrogen are required?

    b) How many moles of ammonia are formed?

4 In a flask we have 5 mol of propane that react with an excess of oxygen according the following equation:

$$C_3H_8 + O_2 \rightarrow CO_2 + H_2O \quad \text{(unbalanced)}$$

Determine:

    a) The volume obtained of carbon dioxide gas at a temperature of 298 °C and a pressure of 2.3 atm.

    b) Mass of water obtained.

5 In a flask we have 3.75 mol of calcium hydroxide that react with a solution 4.3 mol/L in hydrochloric acid according the following equation:

$$2HCl + Ca(OH)_2 \rightarrow CaCl_2 + 2H_2O$$

Find:

    a) Volume of hydrochloric acid solution required.

    b) Mass of water formed.

6 In a receptacle we have 455 g of carbon dioxide that react with an excess of hydrogen according the following equation:

$$CO_2 + H_2 \rightarrow CO + H_2O$$

Determine:

    a) The volume obtained of carbon monoxide gas at a temperature of 295 °C and a pressure of 3 atm.

    b) Mass of water obtained.

7 In a receptacle we have 14 g of sulfuric acid that react with an excess of zinc according the following equation:

$$H_2SO_4 + Zn \rightarrow ZnSO_4 + H_2$$

Find:

a) The volume obtained of hydrogen gas at a temperature of 294 °C and a pressure of 9.6 atm.

b) Mass of zinc sulfate obtained.

8 In a flask we have 5 mol of methane that react with an excess of oxygen according the following equation:

$$CH_4 + 2O_2 \rightarrow CO_2 + 2H_2O$$

Determine:

a) The volume obtained of carbon dioxide gas at a temperature of 0 °C and a pressure of 1 atm.

b) Mass of water formed.

9 In a flask we have 2036 mL of solution 1.3 mol/L in ammonia that react with an excess of hydrogen chloride according the following equation:

$$NH_3 + HCl \rightarrow NH_4Cl$$

Find:

a) Mass of ammonium chloride obtained.

b) How many moles of ammonium chloride are obtained?

10 In a flask we have 354.2 mL of solution 2.8 mol/L in phosphoric acid that react with an excess of zinc according the following equation:

$$2H_3PO_4 + 3Zn \rightarrow Zn_3(PO_4)_2 + 3H_2$$

Determine:

a) The volume obtained of hydrogen gas at a temperature of 260 °C and a pressure of 1 atm.

b) Mass of zinc phosphate formed.

11 In a balloon flask we have 485 mL of solution 1.8 mol/L in potassium hydroxide that react with a solution 1.8 mol/L in nitric acid according the following equation:

$$HNO_3 + KOH \rightarrow KNO_3 + H_2O$$

Calculate:

a) Volume needed of nitric acid solution.

b) Mass of potassium nitrate obtained.

12 In a receptacle we have 225 g of chloric acid with a percent purity of 52 % that react with an excess of lithium hydroxide according the following equation:

$$HClO_3 + LiOH \rightarrow LiClO_3 + H_2O$$

Calculate:

a) Mass of lithium chlorate obtained.

b) How many moles of water are formed?

13 In a receptacle we have 58 g of sulfuric acid with a percent purity of 88 % that react with an excess of zinc according the following equation:

$$H_2SO_4 + Zn \rightarrow ZnSO_4 + H_2$$

Calculate:

    a) The volume obtained of hydrogen gas at a temperature of 53 °C and a pressure of 7.7 atm.

    b) Mass of zinc sulfate formed.

14 In a balloon flask we have 14.71 g of lithium hydroxide that react with a solution 0.3 mol/L in chloric acid according the following equation:

$$HClO_3 + LiOH \rightarrow LiClO_3 + H_2O$$

Determine:

    a) Volume needed of chloric acid solution.

    b) Mass of water formed.

15 We want obtain 63 g of water. For that, we react nitric acid with an excess of potassium hydroxide according the following equation:

$$HNO_3 + KOH \rightarrow KNO_3 + H_2O$$

Find:

    a) How many moles of nitric acid are required?

    b) How many moles of potassium nitrate are obtained?

16 In a balloon flask we have 122.8 L of propane gas at a temperature of 96 °C and a pressure of 5.9 atm that react with an excess of oxygen according the following equation:

$$C_3H_8 + O_2 \rightarrow CO_2 + H_2O \quad \text{(not balanced)}$$

Find:

    a) Mass of water obtained.

    b) How many moles of carbon dioxide are formed?

17 In a flask we have 1.433 mol of aluminum hydroxide that react with a solution 3.3 mol/L in hydrochloric acid according the following equation:

$$3HCl + Al(OH)_3 \rightarrow AlCl_3 + 3H_2O$$

Find:

    a) Volume of hydrochloric acid solution required.

    b) Mass of aluminum chloride obtained.

18 We want obtain 117.7 g of water. For that, we react hydrogen gas at a temperature of 0 °C and a pressure of 1 atm with an excess of oxygen according the following equation:

$$2H_2 + O_2 \rightarrow 2H_2O$$

Calculate:

    a) Volume required of hydrogen gas at a temperature of 0 °C and a pressure of 1 atm.

    b) How many moles of water are formed?

19 In a balloon flask we have 166.9 L of carbon dioxide gas at a temperature of 0 °C and a pressure of 1 atm that react with an excess of hydrogen according the following equation:

$$CO_2 + H_2 \rightarrow CO + H_2O$$

Determine:

a) The volume obtained of carbon monoxide gas at a temperature of 0 °C and a pressure of 1 atm.

b) Mass of water formed.

20 In a flask we have 348.4 L of ammonia gas at a temperature of 60 °C and a pressure of 6.9 atm that react with a solution 4.3 mol/L in sulfuric acid according the following equation:

$$H_2SO_4 + 2NH_3 \rightarrow (NH_4)_2SO_4$$

Find:

a) Volume needed of sulfuric acid solution.

b) Mass of ammonium sulfate formed.

21 We want obtain 59.74 g of aluminum chloride. For that, we react hydrochloric acid with an excess of aluminum according the following equation:

$$HCl + Al \rightarrow AlCl_3 + H_2 \quad \text{(unbalanced)}$$

Calculate:

a) Mass of hydrochloric acid required.

b) How many moles of hydrogen are formed?

22 In a receptacle we have 55 g of hydrogen with a percent purity of 61 % that react with an excess of nitrogen according the following equation:

$$3H_2 + N_2 \rightarrow 2NH_3$$

Calculate:

a) The volume obtained of ammonia gas at a temperature of 0 °C and a pressure of 1 atm.

b) Mass of ammonia formed.

23 In a balloon flask we have 131.3 mL of solution 4.8 mol/L in sodium hydroxide that react with a solution 2.3 mol/L in sulfuric acid according the following equation:

$$H_2SO_4 + 2NaOH \rightarrow Na_2SO_4 + 2H_2O$$

Find:

a) Volume of sulfuric acid solution required.

b) Mass of sodium sulfate formed.

24 In a receptacle we have 80 g of hydrochloric acid that react with an excess of aluminum according the following equation:

$$6HCl + 2Al \rightarrow 2AlCl_3 + 3H_2$$

Calculate:

a) Mass of aluminum chloride obtained.

b) How many moles of hydrogen are obtained?

25 In a receptacle we have 16 g of carbon dioxide with a percent purity of 63 % that react with an excess of hydrogen according the following equation:

$$CO_2 + H_2 \rightarrow CO + H_2O$$

Find:

    a) The volume obtained of carbon monoxide gas at a temperature of 329 °C and a pressure of 1 atm.

    b) Mass of water formed.

26 In a balloon flask we have 45.03 g of zinc that react with a solution 3.8 mol/L in phosphoric acid according the following equation:

$$H_3PO_4 + Zn \rightarrow Zn_3(PO_4)_2 + H_2 \quad \text{(not balanced)}$$

Determine:

    a) Volume needed of phosphoric acid solution.

    b) Mass of hydrogen obtained.

27 We want obtain 156.6 g of water. For that, we react carbon dioxide with a percent purity of 79 % with an excess of hydrogen according the following equation:

$$CO_2 + H_2 \rightarrow CO + H_2O$$

Determine:

    a) How many moles of carbon dioxide are required?

    b) How many moles of carbon monoxide are obtained?

28 In a flask we have 4.1 mol of propane that react with an excess of oxygen according the following equation:

$$C_3H_8 + O_2 \rightarrow CO_2 + H_2O \quad \text{(not balanced)}$$

Calculate:

    a) The volume obtained of carbon dioxide gas at a temperature of 0 °C and a pressure of 1 atm.

    b) Mass of water formed.

29 In a flask we have 17.2 mol of ammonia that react with a solution 1.8 mol/L in sulfuric acid according the following equation:

$$H_2SO_4 + 2NH_3 \rightarrow (NH_4)_2SO_4$$

Determine:

    a) Volume needed of sulfuric acid solution.

    b) Mass of ammonium sulfate formed.

30 In a balloon flask we have 4.7 L of methane gas at a temperature of 328 °C and a pressure of 1 atm that react with an excess of oxygen according the following equation:

$$CH_4 + 2O_2 \rightarrow CO_2 + 2H_2O$$

Find:

    a) Mass of water formed.

    b) How many moles of carbon dioxide are formed?

31 In a balloon flask we have 123.9 L of carbon dioxide gas at a temperature of 0 °C and a pressure of 1 atm that react with an excess of hydrogen according the following equation:

$$CO_2 + H_2 \rightarrow CO + H_2O$$

Determine:

    a) The volume obtained of carbon monoxide gas at a temperature of 0 °C and a pressure of 1 atm.

    b) Mass of water formed.

32 In a flask we have 148.2 L of carbon dioxide gas at a temperature of 106 °C and a pressure of 1 atm that react with a solution 3.3 mol/L in sodium hydroxide according the following equation:

$$NaOH + CO_2 \rightarrow NaHCO_3$$

Determine:

    a) Volume needed of sodium hydroxide solution.

    b) Mass of sodium bicarbonate obtained.

33 In a receptacle we have 41 g of phosphoric acid that react with an excess of zinc according the following equation:

$$2H_3PO_4 + 3Zn \rightarrow Zn_3(PO_4)_2 + 3H_2$$

Determine:

    a) The volume obtained of hydrogen gas at a temperature of 25 °C and a pressure of 2.7 atm.

    b) Mass of zinc phosphate formed.

34 In a flask we have 95.24 mL of solution 3.3 mol/L in phosphoric acid that react with an excess of aluminum according the following equation:

$$2H_3PO_4 + 2Al \rightarrow 2AlPO_4 + 3H_2$$

Find:

    a) The volume obtained of hydrogen gas at a temperature of 25 °C and a pressure of 1 atm.

    b) Mass of aluminum phosphate formed.

35 In a balloon flask we have 339.3 mL of solution 0.8 mol/L in sodium hydroxide that react with a solution 1.3 mol/L in sulfuric acid according the following equation:

$$H_2SO_4 + NaOH \rightarrow Na_2SO_4 + H_2O \quad \text{(not balanced)}$$

Find:

    a) Volume needed of sulfuric acid solution.

    b) Mass of water obtained.

36 We want obtain 175.7 g of ammonia. For that, we react hydrogen with an excess of nitrogen according the following equation:

$$H_2 + N_2 \rightarrow NH_3 \quad \text{(not balanced)}$$

Find:

    a) Mass of hydrogen required.

    b) How many moles of ammonia are obtained?

37 In a receptacle we have 36 g of hydrochloric acid with a percent purity of 64 % that react with an excess of aluminum according the following equation:

$$6HCl + 2Al \rightarrow 2AlCl_3 + 3H_2$$

Find:

    a) The volume obtained of hydrogen gas at a temperature of 25 °C and a pressure of 1 atm.

    b) Mass of aluminum chloride formed.

38 In a balloon flask we have 17.51 g of aluminum hydroxide that react with a solution 3.3 mol/L in sulfuric acid according the following equation:

$$H_2SO_4 + Al(OH)_3 \rightarrow Al_2(SO_4)_3 + H_2O \quad \text{(not balanced)}$$

Calculate:

    a) Volume of sulfuric acid solution required.

    b) Mass of aluminum sulfate formed.

39 We want obtain 17.8 g of aluminum chloride. For that, we react hydrochloric acid with an excess of aluminum hydroxide according the following equation:

$$3HCl + Al(OH)_3 \rightarrow AlCl_3 + 3H_2O$$

Determine:

    a) How many moles of hydrochloric acid are required?

    b) How many moles of water are formed?

40 In a flask we have 2.2 mol of phosphoric acid that react with an excess of zinc according the following equation:

$$H_3PO_4 + Zn \rightarrow Zn_3(PO_4)_2 + H_2 \quad \text{(unbalanced)}$$

Determine:

    a) The volume obtained of hydrogen gas at a temperature of 25 °C and a pressure of 1 atm.

    b) Mass of zinc phosphate obtained.

41 In a flask we have 1.9 mol of aluminum that react with a solution 1.3 mol/L in phosphoric acid according the following equation:

$$H_3PO_4 + Al \rightarrow AlPO_4 + H_2 \quad \text{(unbalanced)}$$

Find:

    a) Volume of phosphoric acid solution required.

    b) Mass of hydrogen formed.

42 We want obtain 533 g of ammonia. For that, we react nitrogen gas at a temperature of 106 °C and a pressure of 7.1 atm with an excess of hydrogen according the following equation:

$$N_2 + H_2 \rightarrow NH_3 \quad \text{(unbalanced)}$$

Find:

    a) Volume required of nitrogen gas at a temperature of 106 °C and a pressure of 7.1 atm.

    b) How many moles of ammonia are obtained?

43 We want obtain 6.391 g of water. For that, we react a solution 4.3 mol/L in chloric acid with an excess of lithium hydroxide according the following equation:

$$HClO_3 + LiOH \rightarrow LiClO_3 + H_2O$$

Find:

    a) Volume of chloric acid solution required.

    b) How many moles of lithium chlorate are obtained?

44 In a balloon flask we have 40.82 g of sodium hydroxide that react with a solution 0.3 mol/L in sulfuric acid according the following equation:

$$H_2SO_4 + 2NaOH \rightarrow Na_2SO_4 + 2H_2O$$

Determine:

    a) Volume of sulfuric acid solution required.

    b) Mass of sodium sulfate obtained.

45 In a flask we have 81 L of carbon dioxide gas at a temperature of 265 °C and a pressure of 7.6 atm that react with a solution 1.3 mol/L in sodium hydroxide according the following equation:

$$NaOH + CO_2 \rightarrow NaHCO_3$$

Find:

    a) Volume needed of sodium hydroxide solution.

    b) Mass of sodium bicarbonate formed.

46 In a flask we have 68.77 mL of solution 2.3 mol/L in sulfuric acid that react with an excess of aluminum according the following equation:

$$H_2SO_4 + Al \rightarrow Al_2(SO_4)_3 + H_2 \quad \text{(not balanced)}$$

Determine:

    a) The volume obtained of hydrogen gas at a temperature of 160 °C and a pressure of 4.8 atm.

    b) Mass of aluminum sulfate formed.

47 In a balloon flask we have 114.7 mL of solution 4.3 mol/L in aluminum hydroxide that react with a solution 1.3 mol/L in hydrochloric acid according the following equation:

$$3HCl + Al(OH)_3 \rightarrow AlCl_3 + 3H_2O$$

Determine:

    a) Volume needed of hydrochloric acid solution.

    b) Mass of aluminum chloride formed.

48 We want obtain 276.5 g of aluminum chloride. For that, we react hydrochloric acid with a percent purity of 54 % with an excess of aluminum according the following equation:

$$6HCl + 2Al \rightarrow 2AlCl_3 + 3H_2$$

Calculate:

    a) Mass of impure hydrochloric acid required.

    b) How many moles of hydrogen are formed?

49 In a balloon flask we have 389 g of sodium hydroxide that react with a solution 4.8 mol/L in hydrochloric acid according the following equation:

$HCl + NaOH \rightarrow NaCl + H_2O$

Determine:
   a) Volume of hydrochloric acid solution required.
   b) Mass of water obtained.

50 In a balloon flask we have 45.03 g of zinc that react with a solution 3.3 mol/L in phosphoric acid according the following equation:

$H_3PO_4 + Zn \rightarrow Zn_3(PO_4)_2 + H_2$ (unbalanced)

Calculate:
   a) Volume of phosphoric acid solution required.
   b) Mass of hydrogen obtained.

51 In a receptacle we have 39 g of methane with a percent purity of 94 % that react with an excess of oxygen according the following equation:

$CH_4 + 2O_2 \rightarrow CO_2 + 2H_2O$

Determine:
   a) The volume obtained of carbon dioxide gas at a temperature of 182 °C and a pressure of 7 atm.
   b) Mass of water formed.

52 In a flask we have 7.4 mol of hydrochloric acid that react with an excess of aluminum according the following equation:

$6HCl + 2Al \rightarrow 2AlCl_3 + 3H_2$

Calculate:
   a) The volume obtained of hydrogen gas at a temperature of 0 °C and a pressure of 1 atm.
   b) Mass of aluminum chloride formed.

53 In a flask we have 2.6 mol of aluminum that react with a solution 0.8 mol/L in phosphoric acid according the following equation:

$H_3PO_4 + Al \rightarrow AlPO_4 + H_2$ (not balanced)

Find:
   a) Volume of phosphoric acid solution required.
   b) Mass of hydrogen formed.

54 In a balloon flask we have 29.92 g of aluminum hydroxide that react with a solution 4.3 mol/L in hydrochloric acid according the following equation:

$3HCl + Al(OH)_3 \rightarrow AlCl_3 + 3H_2O$

Determine:
   a) Volume of hydrochloric acid solution required.
   b) Mass of aluminum chloride obtained.

55 In a balloon flask we have 159.1 L of propane gas at a temperature of 82 °C and a pressure of 8.8 atm that react with an excess of oxygen according the following equation:

$$C_3H_8 + 5O_2 \rightarrow 3CO_2 + 4H_2O$$

Calculate:

    a) The volume obtained of carbon dioxide gas at a temperature of 82 °C and a pressure of 8.8 atm.

    b) Mass of water formed.

56 In a flask we have 120.8 L of hydrogen chloride gas at a temperature of 25 °C and a pressure of 1 atm that react with a solution 3.8 mol/L in ammonia according the following equation:

$$NH_3 + HCl \rightarrow NH_4Cl$$

Determine:

    a) Volume needed of ammonia solution.

    b) Mass of ammonium chloride formed.

57 We want obtain 25.61 g of zinc phosphate. For that, we react a solution 2.8 mol/L in phosphoric acid with an excess of zinc according the following equation:

$$2H_3PO_4 + 3Zn \rightarrow Zn_3(PO_4)_2 + 3H_2$$

Find:

    a) Volume needed of phosphoric acid solution.

    b) How many moles of hydrogen are obtained?

58 In a flask we have 158.4 mL of solution 2.3 mol/L in hydrochloric acid that react with an excess of aluminum according the following equation:

$$HCl + Al \rightarrow AlCl_3 + H_2 \quad \text{(not balanced)}$$

Find:

    a) The volume obtained of hydrogen gas at a temperature of 314 °C and a pressure of 1 atm.

    b) Mass of aluminum chloride obtained.

59 In a balloon flask we have 55.81 mL of solution 1.8 mol/L in aluminum hydroxide that react with a solution 3.8 mol/L in hydrochloric acid according the following equation:

$$3HCl + Al(OH)_3 \rightarrow AlCl_3 + 3H_2O$$

Find:

    a) Volume needed of hydrochloric acid solution.

    b) Mass of water formed.

60 We want obtain 29.55 g of zinc phosphate. For that, we react phosphoric acid with an excess of zinc according the following equation:

$$H_3PO_4 + Zn \rightarrow Zn_3(PO_4)_2 + H_2 \quad \text{(unbalanced)}$$

Determine:

    a) Mass of phosphoric acid required.

    b) How many moles of hydrogen are obtained?

61 In a receptacle we have 43 g of nitrogen with a percent purity of 60 % that react with an excess of hydrogen according the following equation:

$$N_2 + 3H_2 \rightarrow 2NH_3$$

Find:

    a) The volume obtained of ammonia gas at a temperature of 306 °C and a pressure of 1 atm.

    b) Mass of ammonia formed.

62 In a balloon flask we have 295.6 mL of solution 3.8 mol/L in sodium hydroxide that react with a solution 2.3 mol/L in hydrochloric acid according the following equation:

$$HCl + NaOH \rightarrow NaCl + H_2O$$

Determine:

    a) Volume needed of hydrochloric acid solution.

    b) Mass of sodium chloride formed.

63 We want obtain 386.1 g of zinc phosphate. For that, we react phosphoric acid with a percent purity of 80 % with an excess of zinc according the following equation:

$$2H_3PO_4 + 3Zn \rightarrow Zn_3(PO_4)_2 + 3H_2$$

Calculate:

    a) How many moles of phosphoric acid are required?

    b) How many moles of hydrogen are obtained?

64 In a flask we have 1.2 mol of hydrochloric acid that react with an excess of zinc according the following equation:

$$2HCl + Zn \rightarrow ZnCl_2 + H_2$$

Find:

    a) The volume obtained of hydrogen gas at a temperature of 319 °C and a pressure of 5.4 atm.

    b) Mass of zinc chloride formed.

65 In a flask we have 3.2 mol of sodium hydroxide that react with a solution 0.8 mol/L in sulfuric acid according the following equation:

$$H_2SO_4 + 2NaOH \rightarrow Na_2SO_4 + 2H_2O$$

Find:

    a) Volume of sulfuric acid solution required.

    b) Mass of sodium sulfate obtained.

66 We want obtain 101.2 g of ammonia. For that, we react hydrogen gas at a temperature of 25 °C and a pressure of 5.3 atm with an excess of nitrogen according the following equation:

$$H_2 + N_2 \rightarrow NH_3 \quad \text{(unbalanced)}$$

Calculate:

    a) Volume required of hydrogen gas at a temperature of 25 °C and a pressure of 5.3 atm.

    b) How many moles of ammonia are obtained?

67 In a balloon flask we have 137.8 L of methane gas at a temperature of 279 °C and a pressure of 8 atm that react with an excess of oxygen according the following equation:

$$CH_4 + 2O_2 \rightarrow CO_2 + 2H_2O$$

Find:

a) The volume obtained of carbon dioxide gas at a temperature of 279 °C and a pressure of 8 atm.

b) Mass of water obtained.

68 In a flask we have 69.8 L of hydrogen chloride gas at a temperature of 0 °C and a pressure of 1 atm that react with a solution 3.8 mol/L in ammonia according the following equation:

$$NH_3 + HCl \rightarrow NH_4Cl$$

Calculate:

a) Volume needed of ammonia solution.

b) Mass of ammonium chloride formed.

69 We want obtain 9.863 g of water. For that, we react a solution 0.8 mol/L in hydrochloric acid with an excess of aluminum hydroxide according the following equation:

$$HCl + Al(OH)_3 \rightarrow AlCl_3 + H_2O \quad \text{(unbalanced)}$$

Find:

a) Volume needed of hydrochloric acid solution.

b) How many moles of aluminum chloride are obtained?

70 In a flask we have 157 mL of solution 1.3 mol/L in phosphoric acid that react with an excess of aluminum according the following equation:

$$2H_3PO_4 + 2Al \rightarrow 2AlPO_4 + 3H_2$$

Find:

a) The volume obtained of hydrogen gas at a temperature of 0 °C and a pressure of 1 atm.

b) Mass of aluminum phosphate formed.

71 In a balloon flask we have 778.9 mL of solution 1.3 mol/L in sodium hydroxide that react with a solution 0.8 mol/L in hydrochloric acid according the following equation:

$$HCl + NaOH \rightarrow NaCl + H_2O$$

Calculate:

a) Volume of hydrochloric acid solution required.

b) Mass of sodium chloride formed.

72 We want obtain 30.86 g of water. For that, we react ethene with an excess of oxygen according the following equation:

$$C_2H_4 + O_2 \rightarrow CO_2 + H_2O \quad \text{(unbalanced)}$$

Calculate:

a) Mass of ethene required.

b) How many moles of carbon dioxide are formed?

73 In a flask we have 0.06667 mol of aluminum that react with a solution 2.3 mol/L in hydrochloric acid according the following equation:

$$HCl + Al \rightarrow AlCl_3 + H_2 \quad \text{(unbalanced)}$$

Find:

    a) Volume needed of hydrochloric acid solution.

    b) Mass of hydrogen obtained.

74 In a balloon flask we have 57.97 g of hydrogen chloride that react with a solution 4.3 mol/L in ammonia according the following equation:

$$NH_3 + HCl \rightarrow NH_4Cl$$

Calculate:

    a) Volume of ammonia solution required.

    b) Mass of ammonium chloride formed.

75 In a flask we have 5.3 mol of sulfuric acid that react with an excess of aluminum hydroxide according the following equation:

$$3H_2SO_4 + 2Al(OH)_3 \rightarrow Al_2(SO_4)_3 + 6H_2O$$

Find:

    a) Mass of water obtained.

    b) How many moles of aluminum sulfate are formed?

76 In a flask we have 2.6 mol of sulfuric acid that react with an excess of zinc according the following equation:

$$H_2SO_4 + Zn \rightarrow ZnSO_4 + H_2$$

Find:

    a) The volume obtained of hydrogen gas at a temperature of 284 °C and a pressure of 1 atm.

    b) Mass of zinc sulfate formed.

77 In a flask we have 5.8 mol of sodium hydroxide that react with a solution 4.3 mol/L in hydrochloric acid according the following equation:

$$HCl + NaOH \rightarrow NaCl + H_2O$$

Determine:

    a) Volume needed of hydrochloric acid solution.

    b) Mass of sodium chloride obtained.

78 We want obtain 16.16 g of water. For that, we react a solution 3.8 mol/L in sulfuric acid with an excess of sodium hydroxide according the following equation:

$$H_2SO_4 + 2NaOH \rightarrow Na_2SO_4 + 2H_2O$$

Calculate:

    a) Volume of sulfuric acid solution required.

    b) How many moles of sodium sulfate are obtained?

79 In a balloon flask we have 183.1 L of propane gas at a temperature of 274 °C and a pressure of 3 atm that react with an excess of oxygen according the following equation:

$$C_3H_8 + 5O_2 \rightarrow 3CO_2 + 4H_2O$$

Calculate:

    a) The volume obtained of carbon dioxide gas at a temperature of 274 °C and a pressure of 3 atm.

    b) Mass of water formed.

80 In a flask we have 141.4 L of carbon dioxide gas at a temperature of 364 °C and a pressure of 6.3 atm that react with a solution 0.8 mol/L in sodium hydroxide according the following equation:

$$NaOH + CO_2 \rightarrow NaHCO_3$$

Find:

    a) Volume needed of sodium hydroxide solution.

    b) Mass of sodium bicarbonate obtained.

81 In a flask we have 199.8 mL of solution 4.8 mol/L in hydrochloric acid that react with an excess of zinc according the following equation:

$$2HCl + Zn \rightarrow ZnCl_2 + H_2$$

Find:

    a) Mass of zinc chloride formed.

    b) How many moles of hydrogen are obtained?

82 In a flask we have 57.82 mL of solution 3.3 mol/L in sulfuric acid that react with an excess of zinc according the following equation:

$$H_2SO_4 + Zn \rightarrow ZnSO_4 + H_2$$

Find:

    a) The volume obtained of hydrogen gas at a temperature of 165 °C and a pressure of 9.7 atm.

    b) Mass of zinc sulfate obtained.

83 In a balloon flask we have 239.9 mL of solution 0.8 mol/L in aluminum hydroxide that react with a solution 1.3 mol/L in sulfuric acid according the following equation:

$$H_2SO_4 + Al(OH)_3 \rightarrow Al_2(SO_4)_3 + H_2O \quad \text{(unbalanced)}$$

Calculate:

    a) Volume of sulfuric acid solution required.

    b) Mass of aluminum sulfate formed.

84 In a balloon flask we have 12.2 g of aluminum hydroxide with a percent purity of 53 % that react with a solution 2.8 mol/L in sulfuric acid according the following equation:

$$3H_2SO_4 + 2Al(OH)_3 \rightarrow Al_2(SO_4)_3 + 6H_2O$$

Determine:

    a) Volume needed of sulfuric acid solution.

    b) Mass of water obtained.

85 In a receptacle we have 57 g of propane that react with an excess of oxygen according the following equation:

$$C_3H_8 + 5O_2 \rightarrow 3CO_2 + 4H_2O$$

Calculate:

    a) The volume obtained of carbon dioxide gas at a temperature of 0 °C and a pressure of 1 atm.

    b) Mass of water formed.

86 In a balloon flask we have 10.25 g of ammonia that react with a solution 2.8 mol/L in hydrochloric acid according the following equation:

$$HCl + NH_3 \rightarrow NH_4Cl$$

Determine:

    a) Volume of hydrochloric acid solution required.

    b) Mass of ammonium chloride obtained.

87 In a flask we have 5.2 mol of sulfuric acid that react with an excess of aluminum hydroxide according the following equation:

$$H_2SO_4 + Al(OH)_3 \rightarrow Al_2(SO_4)_3 + H_2O \quad \text{(unbalanced)}$$

Determine:

    a) Mass of water formed.

    b) How many moles of aluminum sulfate are obtained?

88 In a flask we have 6.8 mol of propane that react with an excess of oxygen according the following equation:

$$C_3H_8 + O_2 \rightarrow CO_2 + H_2O \quad \text{(unbalanced)}$$

Calculate:

    a) The volume obtained of carbon dioxide gas at a temperature of 308 °C and a pressure of 1.2 atm.

    b) Mass of water formed.

89 In a flask we have 8.4 mol of ammonia that react with a solution 4.3 mol/L in hydrochloric acid according the following equation:

$$HCl + NH_3 \rightarrow NH_4Cl$$

Determine:

    a) Volume of hydrochloric acid solution required.

    b) Mass of ammonium chloride formed.

90 We want obtain 66 g of water. For that, we react hydrogen gas at a temperature of 371 °C and a pressure of 1 atm with an excess of oxygen according the following equation:

$$2H_2 + O_2 \rightarrow 2H_2O$$

Find:

    a) Volume required of hydrogen gas at a temperature of 371 °C and a pressure of 1 atm.

    b) How many moles of water are formed?

91 We want obtain 66 g of ammonium sulfate. For that, we react sulfuric acid with a percent purity of 80 % with an excess of ammonia according the following equation:

$H_2SO_4 + NH_3 \rightarrow (NH_4)_2SO_4$ (unbalanced)

Find:

    a) How many moles of sulfuric acid are required?

    b) How many moles of ammonium sulfate are obtained?

92 In a flask we have 2.1 mol of zinc that react with a solution 1.3 mol/L in hydrochloric acid according the following equation:

$2HCl + Zn \rightarrow ZnCl_2 + H_2$

Calculate:

    a) Volume needed of hydrochloric acid solution.

    b) Mass of hydrogen formed.

93 In a flask we have 219.8 mL of solution 1.3 mol/L in sulfuric acid that react with an excess of aluminum hydroxide according the following equation:

$H_2SO_4 + Al(OH)_3 \rightarrow Al_2(SO_4)_3 + H_2O$ (unbalanced)

Find:

    a) Mass of water obtained.

    b) How many moles of aluminum sulfate are formed?

94 In a balloon flask we have 153.8 L of hydrogen gas at a temperature of 25 °C and a pressure of 1 atm that react with an excess of nitrogen according the following equation:

$H_2 + N_2 \rightarrow NH_3$ (not balanced)

Find:

    a) The volume obtained of ammonia gas at a temperature of 25 °C and a pressure of 1 atm.

    b) Mass of ammonia obtained.

95 In a balloon flask we have 301.6 mL of solution 1.3 mol/L in calcium hydroxide that react with a solution 2.3 mol/L in hydrochloric acid according the following equation:

$HCl + Ca(OH)_2 \rightarrow CaCl_2 + H_2O$ (unbalanced)

Find:

    a) Volume of hydrochloric acid solution required.

    b) Mass of calcium chloride formed.

96 We want obtain 345.9 g of sodium bicarbonate. For that, we react sodium hydroxide with a percent purity of 61 % with an excess of carbon dioxide according the following equation:

$NaOH + CO_2 \rightarrow NaHCO_3$

Calculate:

    a) Mass of impure sodium hydroxide required.

    b) How many moles of sodium bicarbonate are obtained?

97 In a flask we have 292 mL of solution 3.8 mol/L in hydrochloric acid that react with an excess of zinc according the following equation:

$HCl + Zn \rightarrow ZnCl_2 + H_2$ (unbalanced)

Determine:

   a) The volume obtained of hydrogen gas at a temperature of 25 °C and a pressure of 9.5 atm.

   b) Mass of zinc chloride formed.

98 In a balloon flask we have 47.64 g of calcium hydroxide with a percent purity of 51 % that react with a solution 1.8 mol/L in hydrochloric acid according the following equation:

$2HCl + Ca(OH)_2 \rightarrow CaCl_2 + 2H_2O$

Find:

   a) Volume of hydrochloric acid solution required.

   b) Mass of water obtained.

99 We want obtain 531.8 g of zinc chloride. For that, we react hydrochloric acid with an excess of zinc according the following equation:

$2HCl + Zn \rightarrow ZnCl_2 + H_2$

Calculate:

   a) How many moles of hydrochloric acid are required?

   b) How many moles of hydrogen are formed?

100 61 g of $H_4P_2O_7$ react with AgBr. Determine:

   a) The balanced chemical equation.

   b) Mass and moles required of AgBr.

   c) Mass and moles of $Ag_4P_2O_7$ obtained.

101 53 g of MgO react with $Cd(NO_3)_2$. Calculate:

   a) The balanced chemical equation.

   b) Mass and moles required of $Cd(NO_3)_2$.

   c) Mass and moles of CdO obtained.

102 39 g of $ZnCO_3$ react with $FeCl_3$. Determine:

   a) The balanced chemical equation.

   b) Mass and moles required of $FeCl_3$.

   c) Mass and moles of $Fe_2(CO_3)_3$ obtained.

103 48 g of H_2SO_4 react with $Fe(NO_3)_3$. Determine:

   a) The balanced chemical equation.

   b) Mass and moles required of $Fe(NO_3)_3$.

   c) Mass and moles of $Fe_2(SO_4)_3$ obtained.

104 71 g of $MgCl_2$ react with Li_2SO_4. Calculate:
  a) The balanced chemical equation.
  b) Mass and moles required of Li_2SO_4.
  c) Mass and moles of $LiCl$ obtained.

105 94 g of MgS react with $Pb(CO_3)_2$. Calculate:
  a) The balanced chemical equation.
  b) Mass and moles required of $Pb(CO_3)_2$.
  c) Mass and moles of PbS_2 obtained.

106 81 g of Al_2S_3 react with H_2CO_3. Find:
  a) The balanced chemical equation.
  b) Mass and moles required of H_2CO_3.
  c) Mass and moles of H_2S obtained.

107 96 g of $FeBr_3$ react with $CaCO_3$. Find:
  a) The balanced chemical equation.
  b) Mass and moles required of $CaCO_3$.
  c) Mass and moles of $CaBr_2$ obtained.

108 48 g of $Fe(ClO)_3$ react with $NaClO_3$. Find:
  a) The balanced chemical equation.
  b) Mass and moles required of $NaClO_3$.
  c) Mass and moles of $NaClO$ obtained.

109 28 g of $Ca(NO_3)_2$ react with CuO. Find:
  a) The balanced chemical equation.
  b) Mass and moles required of CuO.
  c) Mass and moles of $Cu(NO_3)_2$ obtained.

110 76 g of $Zn(OH)_2$ react with PbO_2. Find:
  a) The balanced chemical equation.
  b) Mass and moles required of PbO_2.
  c) Mass and moles of $Pb(OH)_4$ obtained.

111 98 g of $PbCl_4$ react with $Fe(NO_3)_3$. Determine:
  a) The balanced chemical equation.
  b) Mass and moles required of $Fe(NO_3)_3$.
  c) Mass and moles of $FeCl_3$ obtained.

112 88 g of $Mg_2P_2O_7$ react with KCl. Find:
  a) The balanced chemical equation.
  b) Mass and moles required of KCl.
  c) Mass and moles of $K_4P_2O_7$ obtained.

113 21 g of Li_2SO_4 react with $Pb(OH)_4$. Find:
  a) The balanced chemical equation.
  b) Mass and moles required of $Pb(OH)_4$.
  c) Mass and moles of $Pb(SO_4)_2$ obtained.

114 30 g of Ag_2O react with K_2CO_3. Calculate:
  a) The balanced chemical equation.
  b) Mass and moles required of K_2CO_3.
  c) Mass and moles of K_2O obtained.

115 34 g of $MgCO_3$ react with $K_4P_2O_7$. Determine:
  a) The balanced chemical equation.
  b) Mass and moles required of $K_4P_2O_7$.
  c) Mass and moles of K_2CO_3 obtained.

116 93 g of Cu_2SO_4 react with $Mg_2P_2O_7$. Find:
  a) The balanced chemical equation.
  b) Mass and moles required of $Mg_2P_2O_7$.
  c) Mass and moles of $MgSO_4$ obtained.

117 69 g of H_2SO_4 react with Cr_2S_3. Determine:
  a) The balanced chemical equation.
  b) Mass and moles required of Cr_2S_3.
  c) Mass and moles of $Cr_2(SO_4)_3$ obtained.

118 94 g of HNO_3 react with Al_2O_3. Determine:
  a) The balanced chemical equation.
  b) Mass and moles required of Al_2O_3.
  c) Mass and moles of $Al(NO_3)_3$ obtained.

119 21 g of $MgCl_2$ react with HClO. Calculate:
  a) The balanced chemical equation.
  b) Mass and moles required of HClO.
  c) Mass and moles of HCl obtained.

120 74 g of HCl react with $Mg(OH)_2$. Find:
   a) The balanced chemical equation.
   b) Mass and moles required of $Mg(OH)_2$.
   c) Mass and moles of $MgCl_2$ obtained.

121 45 g of $MgCl_2$ react with $Fe_2(SO_4)_3$. Calculate:
   a) The balanced chemical equation.
   b) Mass and moles required of $Fe_2(SO_4)_3$.
   c) Mass and moles of $FeCl_3$ obtained.

122 60 g of AgCl react with $Pb(OH)_4$. Calculate:
   a) The balanced chemical equation.
   b) Mass and moles required of $Pb(OH)_4$.
   c) Mass and moles of $PbCl_4$ obtained.

123 91 g of $Zn(NO_3)_2$ react with KI. Find:
   a) The balanced chemical equation.
   b) Mass and moles required of KI.
   c) Mass and moles of KNO_3 obtained.

124 20 g of $Cu(NO_3)_2$ react with $Zn(OH)_2$. Calculate:
   a) The balanced chemical equation.
   b) Mass and moles required of $Zn(OH)_2$.
   c) Mass and moles of $Zn(NO_3)_2$ obtained.

125 71 g of $Cr(OH)_3$ react with CuCl. Calculate:
   a) The balanced chemical equation.
   b) Mass and moles required of CuCl.
   c) Mass and moles of CuOH obtained.

126 83 g of FeO react with AlF_3. Find:
   a) The balanced chemical equation.
   b) Mass and moles required of AlF_3.
   c) Mass and moles of Al_2O_3 obtained.

127 30 g of H_2CO_3 react with Ag_2O. Determine:
   a) The balanced chemical equation.
   b) Mass and moles required of Ag_2O.
   c) Mass and moles of Ag_2CO_3 obtained.

128 73 g of Li_2SO_4 react with $Cu(OH)_2$. Find:
  a) The balanced chemical equation.
  b) Mass and moles required of $Cu(OH)_2$.
  c) Mass and moles of $CuSO_4$ obtained.

129 65 g of Cu_2SO_4 react with $NaNO_3$. Find:
  a) The balanced chemical equation.
  b) Mass and moles required of $NaNO_3$.
  c) Mass and moles of Na_2SO_4 obtained.

130 29 g of $PbCl_4$ react with CdO. Find:
  a) The balanced chemical equation.
  b) Mass and moles required of CdO.
  c) Mass and moles of $CdCl_2$ obtained.

131 66 g of ZnO react with $Al(NO_3)_3$. Determine:
  a) The balanced chemical equation.
  b) Mass and moles required of $Al(NO_3)_3$.
  c) Mass and moles of Al_2O_3 obtained.

132 42 g of KOH react with $Al_2(CO_3)_3$. Calculate:
  a) The balanced chemical equation.
  b) Mass and moles required of $Al_2(CO_3)_3$.
  c) Mass and moles of $Al(OH)_3$ obtained.

133 45 g of $LiCl$ react with $Mg(OH)_2$. Find:
  a) The balanced chemical equation.
  b) Mass and moles required of $Mg(OH)_2$.
  c) Mass and moles of $MgCl_2$ obtained.

134 100 g of CaS react with Fe_2O_3. Find:
  a) The balanced chemical equation.
  b) Mass and moles required of Fe_2O_3.
  c) Mass and moles of Fe_2S_3 obtained.

135 69 g of CuO react with $ZnSO_4$. Calculate:
  a) The balanced chemical equation.
  b) Mass and moles required of $ZnSO_4$.
  c) Mass and moles of ZnO obtained.

136 56 g of CuI react with $Al(OH)_3$. Calculate:

   a) The balanced chemical equation.

   b) Mass and moles required of $Al(OH)_3$.

   c) Mass and moles of AlI_3 obtained.

137 71 g of $CaSO_4$ react with HCl. Find:

   a) The balanced chemical equation.

   b) Mass and moles required of HCl.

   c) Mass and moles of H_2SO_4 obtained.

138 57 g of $Cr_2(SO_4)_3$ react with AgCl. Calculate:

   a) The balanced chemical equation.

   b) Mass and moles required of AgCl.

   c) Mass and moles of Ag_2SO_4 obtained.

139 38 g of $PbCl_4$ react with $Cu_4P_2O_7$. Find:

   a) The balanced chemical equation.

   b) Mass and moles required of $Cu_4P_2O_7$.

   c) Mass and moles of CuCl obtained.

140 47 g of $Mg(OH)_2$ react with $Fe_2(CO_3)_3$. Determine:

   a) The balanced chemical equation.

   b) Mass and moles required of $Fe_2(CO_3)_3$.

   c) Mass and moles of $Fe(OH)_3$ obtained.

141 22 g of $Al_2(CO_3)_3$ react with $Pb(OH)_4$. Determine:

   a) The balanced chemical equation.

   b) Mass and moles required of $Pb(OH)_4$.

   c) Mass and moles of $Pb(CO_3)_2$ obtained.

142 66 g of Na_2SO_4 react with HBr. Find:

   a) The balanced chemical equation.

   b) Mass and moles required of HBr.

   c) Mass and moles of H_2SO_4 obtained.

143 67 g of $Cu_3(PO_4)_2$ react with Ag_2O. Calculate:

   a) The balanced chemical equation.

   b) Mass and moles required of Ag_2O.

   c) Mass and moles of Ag_3PO_4 obtained.

144 70 g of $AgNO_3$ react with H_2CO_3. Calculate:
   a) The balanced chemical equation.
   b) Mass and moles required of H_2CO_3.
   c) Mass and moles of HNO_3 obtained.

145 50 g of CuO react with $Ca(ClO_2)_2$. Calculate:
   a) The balanced chemical equation.
   b) Mass and moles required of $Ca(ClO_2)_2$.
   c) Mass and moles of CaO obtained.

146 48 g of $Pb(SO_4)_2$ react with ZnO. Find:
   a) The balanced chemical equation.
   b) Mass and moles required of ZnO.
   c) Mass and moles of $ZnSO_4$ obtained.

147 64 g of K_2SO_4 react with HCl. Calculate:
   a) The balanced chemical equation.
   b) Mass and moles required of HCl.
   c) Mass and moles of H_2SO_4 obtained.

148 38 g of H_2SO_4 react with KOH. Determine:
   a) The balanced chemical equation.
   b) Mass and moles required of KOH.
   c) Mass and moles of K_2SO_4 obtained.

149 70 g of H_2CO_3 react with $CuOH$. Determine:
   a) The balanced chemical equation.
   b) Mass and moles required of $CuOH$.
   c) Mass and moles of Cu_2CO_3 obtained.

150 96 g of $Al(OH)_3$ react with FeO. Find:
   a) The balanced chemical equation.
   b) Mass and moles required of FeO.
   c) Mass and moles of $Fe(OH)_2$ obtained.

151 94 g of HCl react with $Al(OH)_3$. Determine:
   a) The balanced chemical equation.
   b) Mass and moles required of $Al(OH)_3$.
   c) Mass and moles of $AlCl_3$ obtained.

152 86 g of Cr_2S_3 react with ZnO. Calculate:
   a) The balanced chemical equation.
   b) Mass and moles required of ZnO.
   c) Mass and moles of ZnS obtained.

153 84 g of K_2S react with $CuSO_4$. Calculate:
   a) The balanced chemical equation.
   b) Mass and moles required of $CuSO_4$.
   c) Mass and moles of CuS obtained.

154 42 g of LiOH react with $Cu(NO_3)_2$. Find:
   a) The balanced chemical equation.
   b) Mass and moles required of $Cu(NO_3)_2$.
   c) Mass and moles of $Cu(OH)_2$ obtained.

155 42 g of CdO react with K_2SO_4. Calculate:
   a) The balanced chemical equation.
   b) Mass and moles required of K_2SO_4.
   c) Mass and moles of K_2O obtained.

156 60 g of CuO react with $Pb(OH)_4$. Calculate:
   a) The balanced chemical equation.
   b) Mass and moles required of $Pb(OH)_4$.
   c) Mass and moles of PbO_2 obtained.

157 40 g of $Mg(ClO_2)_2$ react with $CaCl_2$. Calculate:
   a) The balanced chemical equation.
   b) Mass and moles required of $CaCl_2$.
   c) Mass and moles of $Ca(ClO_2)_2$ obtained.

158 31 g of $Mg(OH)_2$ react with CaS. Determine:
   a) The balanced chemical equation.
   b) Mass and moles required of CaS.
   c) Mass and moles of $Ca(OH)_2$ obtained.

159 85 g of $FeCl_2$ react with Ag_2SO_4. Find:
   a) The balanced chemical equation.
   b) Mass and moles required of Ag_2SO_4.
   c) Mass and moles of AgCl obtained.

160 89 g of $CuCl_2$ react with $Cr_2(SO_4)_3$. Calculate:
  a) The balanced chemical equation.
  b) Mass and moles required of $Cr_2(SO_4)_3$.
  c) Mass and moles of $CrCl_3$ obtained.

161 59 g of HCl react with $Ca(NO_3)_2$. Find:
  a) The balanced chemical equation.
  b) Mass and moles required of $Ca(NO_3)_2$.
  c) Mass and moles of $CaCl_2$ obtained.

162 49 g of $Cr(NO_3)_3$ react with CuCl. Calculate:
  a) The balanced chemical equation.
  b) Mass and moles required of CuCl.
  c) Mass and moles of $CuNO_3$ obtained.

163 81 g of KCl react with Li_2CO_3. Calculate:
  a) The balanced chemical equation.
  b) Mass and moles required of Li_2CO_3.
  c) Mass and moles of LiCl obtained.

164 21 g of $AlPO_4$ react with $Ca(NO_3)_2$. Calculate:
  a) The balanced chemical equation.
  b) Mass and moles required of $Ca(NO_3)_2$.
  c) Mass and moles of $Ca_3(PO_4)_2$ obtained.

165 75 g of $CuCO_3$ react with Li_2S. Find:
  a) The balanced chemical equation.
  b) Mass and moles required of Li_2S.
  c) Mass and moles of Li_2CO_3 obtained.

166 95 g of $FeBr_2$ react with $CuCO_3$. Find:
  a) The balanced chemical equation.
  b) Mass and moles required of $CuCO_3$.
  c) Mass and moles of $CuBr_2$ obtained.

167 47 g of $Fe(ClO)_2$ react with $Ca(ClO_3)_2$. Find:
  a) The balanced chemical equation.
  b) Mass and moles required of $Ca(ClO_3)_2$.
  c) Mass and moles of $Ca(ClO)_2$ obtained.

168 27 g of $LiNO_3$ react with K_2O. Find:

a) The balanced chemical equation.

b) Mass and moles required of K_2O.

c) Mass and moles of KNO_3 obtained.

169 59 g of $Cr(OH)_3$ react with $Al(NO_3)_3$. Calculate:

a) The balanced chemical equation.

b) Mass and moles required of $Al(NO_3)_3$.

c) Mass and moles of $Al(OH)_3$ obtained.

170 51 g of $CuCl_2$ react with Na_2S. Calculate:

a) The balanced chemical equation.

b) Mass and moles required of Na_2S.

c) Mass and moles of $NaCl$ obtained.

171 79 g of H_2SO_4 react with $Cr_2(CO_3)_3$. Calculate:

a) The balanced chemical equation.

b) Mass and moles required of $Cr_2(CO_3)_3$.

c) Mass and moles of $Cr_2(SO_4)_3$ obtained.

172 36 g of $Mg(OH)_2$ react with $Cu(ClO_2)_2$. Calculate:

a) The balanced chemical equation.

b) Mass and moles required of $Cu(ClO_2)_2$.

c) Mass and moles of $Cu(OH)_2$ obtained.

173 97 g of Al_2O_3 react with $Zn_2P_2O_7$. Find:

a) The balanced chemical equation.

b) Mass and moles required of $Zn_2P_2O_7$.

c) Mass and moles of ZnO obtained.

174 61 g of $CuCl_2$ react with H_2SO_4. Calculate:

a) The balanced chemical equation.

b) Mass and moles required of H_2SO_4.

c) Mass and moles of HCl obtained.

175 87 g of $CuClO_2$ react with $Al(OH)_3$. Find:

a) The balanced chemical equation.

b) Mass and moles required of $Al(OH)_3$.

c) Mass and moles of $Al(ClO_2)_3$ obtained.

176 96 g of $CuClO_2$ react with HNO_3. Find:
    a) The balanced chemical equation.
    b) Mass and moles required of HNO_3.
    c) Mass and moles of $HClO_2$ obtained.

177 54 g of $Ca(OH)_2$ react with $Cr_2(CO_3)_3$. Find:
    a) The balanced chemical equation.
    b) Mass and moles required of $Cr_2(CO_3)_3$.
    c) Mass and moles of $Cr(OH)_3$ obtained.

178 29 g of H_2S react with $AgOH$. Determine:
    a) The balanced chemical equation.
    b) Mass and moles required of $AgOH$.
    c) Mass and moles of Ag_2S obtained.

179 33 g of $CuCO_3$ react with $LiCl$. Calculate:
    a) The balanced chemical equation.
    b) Mass and moles required of $LiCl$.
    c) Mass and moles of Li_2CO_3 obtained.

180 49 g of $Al(OH)_3$ react with $Fe(NO_3)_3$. Determine:
    a) The balanced chemical equation.
    b) Mass and moles required of $Fe(NO_3)_3$.
    c) Mass and moles of $Fe(OH)_3$ obtained.

181 78 g of $CuClO$ react with Li_2CO_3. Find:
    a) The balanced chemical equation.
    b) Mass and moles required of Li_2CO_3.
    c) Mass and moles of $LiClO$ obtained.

182 93 g of $CaCO_3$ react with HNO_3. Find:
    a) The balanced chemical equation.
    b) Mass and moles required of HNO_3.
    c) Mass and moles of H_2CO_3 obtained.

183 45 g of HCl react with $Zn(OH)_2$. Determine:
    a) The balanced chemical equation.
    b) Mass and moles required of $Zn(OH)_2$.
    c) Mass and moles of $ZnCl_2$ obtained.

184 60 g of PbO_2 react with $Cu(OH)_2$. Find:
  a) The balanced chemical equation.
  b) Mass and moles required of $Cu(OH)_2$.
  c) Mass and moles of CuO obtained.

185 92 g of $Pb_3(PO_4)_4$ react with $LiOH$. Find:
  a) The balanced chemical equation.
  b) Mass and moles required of $LiOH$.
  c) Mass and moles of Li_3PO_4 obtained.

186 38 g of $FeCl_2$ react with Al_2O_3. Find:
  a) The balanced chemical equation.
  b) Mass and moles required of Al_2O_3.
  c) Mass and moles of $AlCl_3$ obtained.

187 49 g of Li_2O react with Al_2S_3. Calculate:
  a) The balanced chemical equation.
  b) Mass and moles required of Al_2S_3.
  c) Mass and moles of Al_2O_3 obtained.

188 23 g of MgO react with $AgNO_3$. Find:
  a) The balanced chemical equation.
  b) Mass and moles required of $AgNO_3$.
  c) Mass and moles of Ag_2O obtained.

189 92 g of $AgCl$ react with H_2SO_4. Calculate:
  a) The balanced chemical equation.
  b) Mass and moles required of H_2SO_4.
  c) Mass and moles of HCl obtained.

190 56 g of $Cr_2(SO_4)_3$ react with $CuNO_3$. Determine:
  a) The balanced chemical equation.
  b) Mass and moles required of $CuNO_3$.
  c) Mass and moles of Cu_2SO_4 obtained.

191 58 g of $Fe(NO_3)_2$ react with Cr_2O_3. Find:
  a) The balanced chemical equation.
  b) Mass and moles required of Cr_2O_3.
  c) Mass and moles of $Cr(NO_3)_3$ obtained.

192 44 g of K_2SO_4 react with $Fe(ClO_2)_3$. Calculate:
   a) The balanced chemical equation.
   b) Mass and moles required of $Fe(ClO_2)_3$.
   c) Mass and moles of $Fe_2(SO_4)_3$ obtained.

193 25 g of LiCl react with $Pb(SO_4)_2$. Find:
   a) The balanced chemical equation.
   b) Mass and moles required of $Pb(SO_4)_2$.
   c) Mass and moles of $PbCl_4$ obtained.

194 29 g of $Cu(ClO)_2$ react with HCl. Determine:
   a) The balanced chemical equation.
   b) Mass and moles required of HCl.
   c) Mass and moles of HClO obtained.

195 31 g of $Cr(OH)_3$ react with $CuNO_3$. Calculate:
   a) The balanced chemical equation.
   b) Mass and moles required of $CuNO_3$.
   c) Mass and moles of CuOH obtained.

196 77 g of CaO react with $ZnSO_4$. Determine:
   a) The balanced chemical equation.
   b) Mass and moles required of $ZnSO_4$.
   c) Mass and moles of ZnO obtained.

197 71 g of $HClO_2$ react with LiCl. Determine:
   a) The balanced chemical equation.
   b) Mass and moles required of LiCl.
   c) Mass and moles of $LiClO_2$ obtained.

198 73 g of AgCl react with $ZnSO_4$. Determine:
   a) The balanced chemical equation.
   b) Mass and moles required of $ZnSO_4$.
   c) Mass and moles of $ZnCl_2$ obtained.

199 In a receptacle we have 29 g of phosphoric acid with a percent purity of 65 % that react with an excess of zinc according the following equation:
$$H_3PO_4 + Zn \rightarrow Zn_3(PO_4)_2 + H_2 \quad \text{(unbalanced)}$$
1.172 L of hydrogen gas are obtained at a temperature of 266 °C and a pressure of 7.3 atm. Determine:
   a) Percent yield of the reaction.
   b) Mass of hydrogen formed.

200 In a balloon flask we have 137.1 L of propane gas at a temperature of 25 °C and a pressure of 4.8 atm that react with an excess of oxygen according the following equation:

$$C_3H_8 + O_2 \rightarrow CO_2 + H_2O \quad \text{(unbalanced)}$$

172.7 L of carbon dioxide gas are obtained at a temperature of 25 °C and a pressure of 4.8 atm. Find:

    a) Percent yield of the reaction.

    b) Mass of carbon dioxide obtained.

201 In a flask we have 7.3 mol of ethene that react with an excess of oxygen according the following equation:

$$C_2H_4 + O_2 \rightarrow CO_2 + H_2O \quad \text{(unbalanced)}$$

The percent yield of the reaction is 57 %. Find:

    a) Mass of water obtained.

    b) How many moles of carbon dioxide are obtained?

202 In a flask we have 0.4 mol of carbon dioxide that react with an excess of hydrogen according the following equation:

$$CO_2 + H_2 \rightarrow CO + H_2O$$

The percent yield of the reaction is 78 %. Find:

    a) The volume obtained of carbon monoxide gas at a temperature of 399 °C and a pressure of 0.7 atm.

    b) Mass of water obtained.

203 In a balloon flask we have 15.2 L of ethene gas at a temperature of 0 °C and a pressure of 1 atm that react with an excess of oxygen according the following equation:

$$C_2H_4 + 3O_2 \rightarrow 2CO_2 + 2H_2O$$

25.23 L of carbon dioxide gas are obtained at a temperature of 0 °C and a pressure of 1 atm. Determine:

    a) Percent yield of the reaction.

    b) Mass of carbon dioxide obtained.

204 In a balloon flask we have 28.7 L of ethene gas at a temperature of 349 °C and a pressure of 6.1 atm that react with an excess of oxygen according the following equation:

$$C_2H_4 + O_2 \rightarrow CO_2 + H_2O \quad \text{(not balanced)}$$

The percent yield of the reaction is 35 %. Calculate:

    a) Mass of water formed.

    b) How many moles of carbon dioxide are formed?

205 In a balloon flask we have 94 L of ethene gas at a temperature of 345 °C and a pressure of 0.6 atm that react with an excess of oxygen according the following equation:

$$C_2H_4 + 3O_2 \rightarrow 2CO_2 + 2H_2O$$

The percent yield of the reaction is 42 %. Calculate:

    a) The volume obtained of carbon dioxide gas at a temperature of 345 °C and a pressure of 0.6 atm.

    b) Mass of water obtained.

206 In a receptacle we have 385 g of phosphoric acid that react with an excess of aluminum according the following equation:

$$2H_3PO_4 + 2Al \rightarrow 2AlPO_4 + 3H_2$$

The percent yield of the reaction is 56 %. Determine:

a) Mass of aluminum phosphate formed.

b) How many moles of hydrogen are obtained?

207 In a receptacle we have 10 g of phosphoric acid that react with an excess of aluminum according the following equation:

$$2H_3PO_4 + 2Al \rightarrow 2AlPO_4 + 3H_2$$

2.779 L of hydrogen gas are obtained at a temperature of 0 °C and a pressure of 1 atm. Determine:

a) Percent yield of the reaction.

b) Mass of hydrogen formed.

208 In a flask we have 2.1 mol of phosphoric acid that react with an excess of zinc according the following equation:

$$H_3PO_4 + Zn \rightarrow Zn_3(PO_4)_2 + H_2 \quad \text{(not balanced)}$$

The percent yield of the reaction is 67 %. Find:

a) Mass of zinc phosphate formed.

b) How many moles of hydrogen are formed?

209 In a flask we have 4.3 mol of ammonia that react with an excess of hydrogen chloride according the following equation:

$$NH_3 + HCl \rightarrow NH_4Cl$$

119.6 g of ammonium chloride are obtained. Determine:

a) Percent yield of the reaction.

210 In a flask we have 6.8 mol of phosphoric acid that react with an excess of aluminum according the following equation:

$$2H_3PO_4 + 2Al \rightarrow 2AlPO_4 + 3H_2$$

11.82 L of hydrogen gas are obtained at a temperature of 25 °C and a pressure of 9.5 atm. Find:

a) Percent yield of the reaction.

b) Mass of hydrogen obtained.

211 In a receptacle we have 345 g of hydrochloric acid that react with an excess of calcium hydroxide according the following equation:

$$2HCl + Ca(OH)_2 \rightarrow CaCl_2 + 2H_2O$$

The percent yield of the reaction is 85 %. Calculate:

a) Mass of water formed.

b) How many moles of calcium chloride are formed?

212 In a balloon flask we have 93.9 L of hydrogen gas at a temperature of 0 °C and a pressure of 1 atm that react with an excess of oxygen according the following equation:

$H_2 + O_2 \rightarrow H_2O$ (not balanced)

50.52 g of water are obtained. Find:

   a) Percent yield of the reaction.

213 In a balloon flask we have 111.6 L of nitrogen gas at a temperature of 25 °C and a pressure of 4.5 atm that react with an excess of hydrogen according the following equation:

$N_2 + 3H_2 \rightarrow 2NH_3$

136.2 L of ammonia gas are obtained at a temperature of 25 °C and a pressure of 4.5 atm. Determine:

   a) Percent yield of the reaction.
   b) Mass of ammonia formed.

214 In a receptacle we have 175 g of chloric acid that react with an excess of lithium hydroxide according the following equation:

$HClO_3 + LiOH \rightarrow LiClO_3 + H_2O$

20.13 g of water are obtained. Find:

   a) Percent yield of the reaction.
   b) Mass of lithium chlorate obtained.

215 In a receptacle we have 11 g of ethene that react with an excess of oxygen according the following equation:

$C_2H_4 + 3O_2 \rightarrow 2CO_2 + 2H_2O$

The percent yield of the reaction is 82 %. Calculate:

   a) The volume obtained of carbon dioxide gas at a temperature of 137 °C and a pressure of 6.6 atm.
   b) Mass of water formed.

216 In a receptacle we have 15 g of hydrochloric acid that react with an excess of calcium hydroxide according the following equation:

$2HCl + Ca(OH)_2 \rightarrow CaCl_2 + 2H_2O$

The percent yield of the reaction is 32 %. Calculate:

   a) Mass of water formed.
   b) How many moles of calcium chloride are obtained?

217 In a flask we have 5.6 mol of phosphoric acid that react with an excess of zinc according the following equation:

$2H_3PO_4 + 3Zn \rightarrow Zn_3(PO_4)_2 + 3H_2$

The percent yield of the reaction is 64 %. Determine:

   a) Mass of zinc phosphate formed.
   b) How many moles of hydrogen are formed?

218 In a flask we have 2.4 mol of nitrogen that react with an excess of hydrogen according the following equation:

$N_2 + H_2 \rightarrow NH_3$ (not balanced)

96.3 L of ammonia gas are obtained at a temperature of 25 °C and a pressure of 1 atm. Determine:
   a) Percent yield of the reaction.
   b) Mass of ammonia obtained.

219 In a flask we have 2.2 mol of hydrochloric acid that react with an excess of ammonia according the following equation:

$HCl + NH_3 \rightarrow NH_4Cl$

71.8 g of ammonium chloride are obtained. Find:
   a) Percent yield of the reaction.

220 In a balloon flask we have 107.8 L of propane gas at a temperature of 0 °C and a pressure of 1 atm that react with an excess of oxygen according the following equation:

$C_3H_8 + 5O_2 \rightarrow 3CO_2 + 4H_2O$

193.9 g of water are obtained. Calculate:
   a) Percent yield of the reaction.
   b) Mass of carbon dioxide formed.

221 In a balloon flask we have 40.8 L of methane gas at a temperature of 0 °C and a pressure of 1 atm that react with an excess of oxygen according the following equation:

$CH_4 + 2O_2 \rightarrow CO_2 + 2H_2O$

33.05 L of carbon dioxide gas are obtained at a temperature of 0 °C and a pressure of 1 atm. Calculate:
   a) Percent yield of the reaction.
   b) Mass of carbon dioxide formed.

222 In a receptacle we have 46 g of hydrochloric acid with a percent purity of 59 % that react with an excess of sodium hydroxide according the following equation:

$HCl + NaOH \rightarrow NaCl + H_2O$

5.354 g of water are obtained. Find:
   a) Percent yield of the reaction.
   b) Mass of sodium chloride formed.

223 In a flask we have 4.7 mol of phosphoric acid that react with an excess of aluminum according the following equation:

$H_3PO_4 + Al \rightarrow AlPO_4 + H_2$ (unbalanced)

The percent yield of the reaction is 58 %. Find:
   a) Mass of aluminum phosphate formed.
   b) How many moles of hydrogen are formed?

224 In a flask we have 0.6 mol of nitrogen that react with an excess of hydrogen according the following equation:

$N_2 + H_2 \rightarrow NH_3$ (not balanced)

16.67 L of ammonia gas are obtained at a temperature of 197 °C and a pressure of 1 atm. Determine:

    a) Percent yield of the reaction.

    b) Mass of ammonia obtained.

225 In a flask we have 4.7 mol of sulfuric acid that react with an excess of zinc according the following equation:

$H_2SO_4 + Zn \rightarrow ZnSO_4 + H_2$

The percent yield of the reaction is 66 %. Find:

    a) Mass of zinc sulfate obtained.

    b) How many moles of hydrogen are obtained?

226 In a flask we have 0.2 mol of hydrochloric acid that react with an excess of zinc according the following equation:

$HCl + Zn \rightarrow ZnCl_2 + H_2$ (unbalanced)

The percent yield of the reaction is 69 %. Find:

    a) The volume obtained of hydrogen gas at a temperature of 25 °C and a pressure of 4.1 atm.

    b) Mass of zinc chloride obtained.

227 In a flask we have 7.8 mol of phosphoric acid that react with an excess of zinc according the following equation:

$2H_3PO_4 + 3Zn \rightarrow Zn_3(PO_4)_2 + 3H_2$

The percent yield of the reaction is 55 %. Find:

    a) The volume obtained of hydrogen gas at a temperature of 292 °C and a pressure of 0.6 atm.

    b) Mass of zinc phosphate formed.

228 In a balloon flask we have 182.4 L of hydrogen gas at a temperature of 25 °C and a pressure of 1 atm that react with an excess of nitrogen according the following equation:

$3H_2 + N_2 \rightarrow 2NH_3$

The percent yield of the reaction is 72 %. Determine:

    a) Mass of ammonia formed.

    b) How many moles of ammonia are formed?

229 In a balloon flask we have 43 L of ethene gas at a temperature of 25 °C and a pressure of 1 atm that react with an excess of oxygen according the following equation:

$C_2H_4 + 3O_2 \rightarrow 2CO_2 + 2H_2O$

31.82 L of carbon dioxide gas are obtained at a temperature of 25 °C and a pressure of 1 atm. Calculate:

    a) Percent yield of the reaction.

    b) Mass of carbon dioxide formed.

230 In a receptacle we have 36 g of hydrogen that react with an excess of nitrogen according the following equation:

$3H_2 + N_2 \rightarrow 2NH_3$

69.36 g of ammonia are obtained. Find:

    a) Percent yield of the reaction.

231 In a receptacle we have 48 g of phosphoric acid that react with an excess of zinc according the following equation:

$H_3PO_4 + Zn \rightarrow Zn_3(PO_4)_2 + H_2$ (not balanced)

1.05 L of hydrogen gas are obtained at a temperature of 98 °C and a pressure of 9.8 atm. Calculate:

    a) Percent yield of the reaction.

    b) Mass of hydrogen formed.

232 In a balloon flask we have 40.7 L of carbon dioxide gas at a temperature of 87 °C and a pressure of 9.5 atm that react with an excess of hydrogen according the following equation:

$CO_2 + H_2 \rightarrow CO + H_2O$

The percent yield of the reaction is 30 %. Calculate:

    a) The volume obtained of carbon monoxide gas at a temperature of 87 °C and a pressure of 9.5 atm.

    b) Mass of water formed.

233 In a flask we have 1.8 mol of nitric acid that react with an excess of potassium hydroxide according the following equation:

$HNO_3 + KOH \rightarrow KNO_3 + H_2O$

The percent yield of the reaction is 31 %. Determine:

    a) Mass of potassium nitrate obtained.

    b) How many moles of water are obtained?

234 In a flask we have 3.8 mol of sulfuric acid that react with an excess of aluminum according the following equation:

$3H_2SO_4 + 2Al \rightarrow Al_2(SO_4)_3 + 3H_2$

66.43 L of hydrogen gas are obtained at a temperature of 0 °C and a pressure of 1 atm. Find:

    a) Percent yield of the reaction.

    b) Mass of hydrogen obtained.

235 In a balloon flask we have 111 L of ethene gas at a temperature of 0 °C and a pressure of 1 atm that react with an excess of oxygen according the following equation:

$C_2H_4 + 3O_2 \rightarrow 2CO_2 + 2H_2O$

186.5 L of carbon dioxide gas are obtained at a temperature of 0 °C and a pressure of 1 atm. Calculate:

    a) Percent yield of the reaction.

    b) Mass of carbon dioxide obtained.

236 In a receptacle we have 40 g of nitric acid with a percent purity of 84 % that react with an excess of potassium hydroxide according the following equation:

$HNO_3 + KOH \rightarrow KNO_3 + H_2O$

The percent yield of the reaction is 43 %. Find:

    a) Mass of potassium nitrate formed.

    b) How many moles of water are formed?

237 In a balloon flask we have 113.2 L of propane gas at a temperature of 25 °C and a pressure of 6.2 atm that react with an excess of oxygen according the following equation:

$C_3H_8 + 5O_2 \rightarrow 3CO_2 + 4H_2O$

681.6 g of water are obtained. Determine:

    a) Percent yield of the reaction.

    b) Mass of carbon dioxide obtained.

238 In a flask we have 3.1 mol of ethene that react with an excess of oxygen according the following equation:

$C_2H_4 + 3O_2 \rightarrow 2CO_2 + 2H_2O$

The percent yield of the reaction is 56 %. Find:

    a) Mass of water obtained.

    b) How many moles of carbon dioxide are obtained?

239 In a receptacle we have 47 g of ethene that react with an excess of oxygen according the following equation:

$C_2H_4 + 3O_2 \rightarrow 2CO_2 + 2H_2O$

The percent yield of the reaction is 50 %. Determine:

    a) The volume obtained of carbon dioxide gas at a temperature of 0 °C and a pressure of 1 atm.

    b) Mass of water formed.

240 In a receptacle we have 255 g of nitrogen with a percent purity of 65 % that react with an excess of hydrogen according the following equation:

$N_2 + H_2 \rightarrow NH_3$ (unbalanced)

The percent yield of the reaction is 31 %. Find:

    a) The volume obtained of ammonia gas at a temperature of 209 °C and a pressure of 6.6 atm.

    b) Mass of ammonia obtained.

241 In a flask we have 8.6 mol of hydrochloric acid that react with an excess of sodium hydroxide according the following equation:

$HCl + NaOH \rightarrow NaCl + H_2O$

105.3 g of water are obtained. Find:

    a) Percent yield of the reaction.

    b) Mass of sodium chloride obtained.

242 In a receptacle we have 39 g of carbon dioxide that react with an excess of hydrogen according the following equation:

$$CO_2 + H_2 \rightarrow CO + H_2O$$

The percent yield of the reaction is 48 %. Find:

    a) The volume obtained of carbon monoxide gas at a temperature of 25 °C and a pressure of 1 atm.

    b) Mass of water obtained.

243 In a flask we have 4.3 mol of sulfuric acid that react with an excess of zinc according the following equation:

$$H_2SO_4 + Zn \rightarrow ZnSO_4 + H_2$$

35.66 L of hydrogen gas are obtained at a temperature of 0 °C and a pressure of 1 atm. Find:

    a) Percent yield of the reaction.

    b) Mass of hydrogen obtained.

244 In a balloon flask we have 84.5 L of hydrogen gas at a temperature of 205 °C and a pressure of 3 atm that react with an excess of nitrogen according the following equation:

$$3H_2 + N_2 \rightarrow 2NH_3$$

46.86 g of ammonia are obtained. Calculate:

    a) Percent yield of the reaction.

245 In a balloon flask we have 148.5 L of carbon dioxide gas at a temperature of 0 °C and a pressure of 1 atm that react with an excess of hydrogen according the following equation:

$$CO_2 + H_2 \rightarrow CO + H_2O$$

51.97 L of carbon monoxide gas are obtained at a temperature of 0 °C and a pressure of 1 atm. Calculate:

    a) Percent yield of the reaction.

    b) Mass of carbon monoxide obtained.

246 In a receptacle we have 10 g of chloric acid with a percent purity of 86 % that react with an excess of lithium hydroxide according the following equation:

$$HClO_3 + LiOH \rightarrow LiClO_3 + H_2O$$

The percent yield of the reaction is 36 %. Calculate:

    a) Mass of water formed.

    b) How many moles of lithium chlorate are formed?

247 In a receptacle we have 52 g of propane that react with an excess of oxygen according the following equation:

$$C_3H_8 + O_2 \rightarrow CO_2 + H_2O \quad \text{(unbalanced)}$$

46.09 L of carbon dioxide gas are obtained at a temperature of 0 °C and a pressure of 1 atm. Determine:

    a) Percent yield of the reaction.

    b) Mass of carbon dioxide obtained.

248 In a receptacle we have 24 g of sulfuric acid that react with an excess of aluminum according the following equation:

$$3H_2SO_4 + 2Al \rightarrow Al_2(SO_4)_3 + 3H_2$$

2.745 L of hydrogen gas are obtained at a temperature of 0 °C and a pressure of 1 atm. Calculate:

    a) Percent yield of the reaction.

    b) Mass of hydrogen obtained.

249 In a flask we have 4.2 mol of sulfuric acid that react with an excess of ammonia according the following equation:

$$H_2SO_4 + NH_3 \rightarrow (NH_4)_2SO_4 \quad \text{(not balanced)}$$

365.9 g of ammonium sulfate are obtained. Calculate:

    a) Percent yield of the reaction.

250 In a flask we have 2.9 mol of sulfuric acid that react with an excess of aluminum according the following equation:

$$H_2SO_4 + Al \rightarrow Al_2(SO_4)_3 + H_2 \quad \text{(not balanced)}$$

41.6 L of hydrogen gas are obtained at a temperature of 0 °C and a pressure of 1 atm. Determine:

    a) Percent yield of the reaction.

    b) Mass of hydrogen formed.

251 In a flask we have 4.5 mol of carbon dioxide that react with an excess of hydrogen according the following equation:

$$CO_2 + H_2 \rightarrow CO + H_2O$$

The percent yield of the reaction is 65 %. Calculate:

    a) The volume obtained of carbon monoxide gas at a temperature of 373 °C and a pressure of 0.6 atm.

    b) Mass of water obtained.

252 In a balloon flask we have 155.8 L of carbon dioxide gas at a temperature of 0 °C and a pressure of 1 atm that react with an excess of hydrogen according the following equation:

$$CO_2 + H_2 \rightarrow CO + H_2O$$

The percent yield of the reaction is 41 %. Determine:

    a) Mass of water formed.

    b) How many moles of carbon monoxide are obtained?

253 In a balloon flask we have 145 L of nitrogen gas at a temperature of 0 °C and a pressure of 1 atm that react with an excess of hydrogen according the following equation:

$$N_2 + H_2 \rightarrow NH_3 \quad \text{(not balanced)}$$

The percent yield of the reaction is 69 %. Calculate:

    a) The volume obtained of ammonia gas at a temperature of 0 °C and a pressure of 1 atm.

    b) Mass of ammonia obtained.

254 In a receptacle we have 22 g of hydrochloric acid that react with an excess of ammonia according the following equation:

$$HCl + NH_3 \rightarrow NH_4Cl$$

25.15 g of ammonium chloride are obtained. Find:

    a) Percent yield of the reaction.

255 In a flask we have 2.7 mol of sulfuric acid that react with an excess of zinc according the following equation:

$$H_2SO_4 + Zn \rightarrow ZnSO_4 + H_2$$

27.84 L of hydrogen gas are obtained at a temperature of 0 °C and a pressure of 1 atm. Calculate:

    a) Percent yield of the reaction.

    b) Mass of hydrogen formed.

256 In a balloon flask we have 91.6 L of carbon dioxide gas at a temperature of 0 °C and a pressure of 1 atm that react with an excess of hydrogen according the following equation:

$$CO_2 + H_2 \rightarrow CO + H_2O$$

27.95 g of water are obtained. Calculate:

    a) Percent yield of the reaction.

    b) Mass of carbon monoxide obtained.

257 In a flask we have 8.4 mol of hydrogen that react with an excess of nitrogen according the following equation:

$$3H_2 + N_2 \rightarrow 2NH_3$$

The percent yield of the reaction is 32 %. Determine:

    a) Mass of ammonia formed.

    b) How many moles of ammonia are formed?

258 In a flask we have 5.2 mol of nitrogen that react with an excess of hydrogen according the following equation:

$$N_2 + H_2 \rightarrow NH_3 \quad \text{(not balanced)}$$

284.1 L of ammonia gas are obtained at a temperature of 25 °C and a pressure of 0.6 atm. Calculate:

    a) Percent yield of the reaction.

    b) Mass of ammonia obtained.

259 In a receptacle we have 11 g of hydrochloric acid that react with an excess of aluminum according the following equation:

$$HCl + Al \rightarrow AlCl_3 + H_2 \quad \text{(not balanced)}$$

The percent yield of the reaction is 37 %. Find:

    a) The volume obtained of hydrogen gas at a temperature of 364 °C and a pressure of 1 atm.

    b) Mass of aluminum chloride formed.

260 In a receptacle we have 300 g of hydrochloric acid that react with an excess of zinc according the following equation:

$$2HCl + Zn \rightarrow ZnCl_2 + H_2$$

The percent yield of the reaction is 49 %. Calculate:

    a) The volume obtained of hydrogen gas at a temperature of 71 °C and a pressure of 9.4 atm.

    b) Mass of zinc chloride obtained.

261 In a balloon flask we have 164.1 L of ethene gas at a temperature of 342 °C and a pressure of 1 atm that react with an excess of oxygen according the following equation:

$$C_2H_4 + 3O_2 \rightarrow 2CO_2 + 2H_2O$$

The percent yield of the reaction is 48 %. Determine:

    a) The volume obtained of carbon dioxide gas at a temperature of 342 °C and a pressure of 1 atm.

    b) Mass of water obtained.

262 In a receptacle we have 180 g of sulfuric acid that react with an excess of sodium hydroxide according the following equation:

$$H_2SO_4 + NaOH \rightarrow Na_2SO_4 + H_2O \quad \text{(unbalanced)}$$

The percent yield of the reaction is 60 %. Find:

    a) Mass of sodium sulfate formed.

    b) How many moles of water are formed?

263 In a receptacle we have 150 g of ethene with a percent purity of 78 % that react with an excess of oxygen according the following equation:

$$C_2H_4 + 3O_2 \rightarrow 2CO_2 + 2H_2O$$

31.19 L of carbon dioxide gas are obtained at a temperature of 66 °C and a pressure of 4.4 atm. Find:

    a) Percent yield of the reaction.

    b) Mass of carbon dioxide formed.

264 In a flask we have 2.6 mol of nitric acid that react with an excess of potassium hydroxide according the following equation:

$$HNO_3 + KOH \rightarrow KNO_3 + H_2O$$

The percent yield of the reaction is 36 %. Calculate:

    a) Mass of water obtained.

    b) How many moles of potassium nitrate are obtained?

265 In a flask we have 7.1 mol of sodium hydroxide that react with an excess of carbon dioxide according the following equation:

$$NaOH + CO_2 \rightarrow NaHCO_3$$

274.3 g of sodium bicarbonate are obtained. Calculate:

    a) Percent yield of the reaction.

266 In a flask we have 6 mol of hydrogen that react with an excess of nitrogen according the following equation:

$H_2 + N_2 \rightarrow NH_3$ (not balanced)

The percent yield of the reaction is 41 %. Calculate:

    a) The volume obtained of ammonia gas at a temperature of 25 °C and a pressure of 1 atm.

    b) Mass of ammonia obtained.

267 In a flask we have 3.4 mol of hydrochloric acid that react with an excess of zinc according the following equation:

$HCl + Zn \rightarrow ZnCl_2 + H_2$ (unbalanced)

7.601 L of hydrogen gas are obtained at a temperature of 25 °C and a pressure of 2.9 atm. Calculate:

    a) Percent yield of the reaction.

    b) Mass of hydrogen formed.

268 In a balloon flask we have 90.2 L of hydrogen gas at a temperature of 0 °C and a pressure of 1 atm that react with an excess of oxygen according the following equation:

$H_2 + O_2 \rightarrow H_2O$ (not balanced)

33.32 g of water are obtained. Determine:

    a) Percent yield of the reaction.

269 In a balloon flask we have 188.6 L of methane gas at a temperature of 292 °C and a pressure of 3.7 atm that react with an excess of oxygen according the following equation:

$CH_4 + 2O_2 \rightarrow CO_2 + 2H_2O$

99.96 L of carbon dioxide gas are obtained at a temperature of 292 °C and a pressure of 3.7 atm. Find:

    a) Percent yield of the reaction.

    b) Mass of carbon dioxide formed.

270 In a receptacle we have 26 g of propane that react with an excess of oxygen according the following equation:

$C_3H_8 + 5O_2 \rightarrow 3CO_2 + 4H_2O$

The percent yield of the reaction is 53 %. Calculate:

    a) Mass of water formed.

    b) How many moles of carbon dioxide are obtained?

271 In a receptacle we have 49 g of sulfuric acid that react with an excess of aluminum according the following equation:

$3H_2SO_4 + 2Al \rightarrow Al_2(SO_4)_3 + 3H_2$

4.037 L of hydrogen gas are obtained at a temperature of 25 °C and a pressure of 1 atm. Find:

    a) Percent yield of the reaction.

    b) Mass of hydrogen formed.

272 In a receptacle we have 27 g of sulfuric acid with a percent purity of 65 % that react with an excess of ammonia according the following equation:

$$H_2SO_4 + 2NH_3 \rightarrow (NH_4)_2SO_4$$

The percent yield of the reaction is 54 %. Calculate:

    a) Mass of ammonium sulfate formed.

    b) How many moles of ammonium sulfate are obtained?

273 In a balloon flask we have 37.3 L of hydrogen gas at a temperature of 321 °C and a pressure of 8.7 atm that react with an excess of oxygen according the following equation:

$$2H_2 + O_2 \rightarrow 2H_2O$$

56.31 g of water are obtained. Calculate:

    a) Percent yield of the reaction.

274 In a flask we have 7.9 mol of carbon dioxide that react with an excess of hydrogen according the following equation:

$$CO_2 + H_2 \rightarrow CO + H_2O$$

The percent yield of the reaction is 33 %. Calculate:

    a) The volume obtained of carbon monoxide gas at a temperature of 25 °C and a pressure of 1 atm.

    b) Mass of water obtained.

275 In a receptacle we have 41 g of sulfuric acid that react with an excess of aluminum according the following equation:

$$H_2SO_4 + Al \rightarrow Al_2(SO_4)_3 + H_2 \quad \text{(unbalanced)}$$

The percent yield of the reaction is 40 %. Determine:

    a) The volume obtained of hydrogen gas at a temperature of 25 °C and a pressure of 3.1 atm.

    b) Mass of aluminum sulfate formed.

276 In a receptacle we have 35 g of methane that react with an excess of oxygen according the following equation:

$$CH_4 + 2O_2 \rightarrow CO_2 + 2H_2O$$

The percent yield of the reaction is 31 %. Calculate:

    a) The volume obtained of carbon dioxide gas at a temperature of 161 °C and a pressure of 1 atm.

    b) Mass of water formed.

277 In a balloon flask we have 129.1 L of nitrogen gas at a temperature of 25 °C and a pressure of 6.5 atm that react with an excess of hydrogen according the following equation:

$$N_2 + 3H_2 \rightarrow 2NH_3$$

108.4 L of ammonia gas are obtained at a temperature of 25 °C and a pressure of 6.5 atm. Determine:

    a) Percent yield of the reaction.

    b) Mass of ammonia formed.

278 In a receptacle we have 420 g of hydrochloric acid that react with an excess of sodium hydroxide according the following equation:

$$HCl + NaOH \rightarrow NaCl + H_2O$$

The percent yield of the reaction is 84 %. Calculate:

    a) Mass of water obtained.

    b) How many moles of sodium chloride are obtained?

279 In a balloon flask we have 101.7 L of ethene gas at a temperature of 25 °C and a pressure of 1 atm that react with an excess of oxygen according the following equation:

$$C_2H_4 + 3O_2 \rightarrow 2CO_2 + 2H_2O$$

The percent yield of the reaction is 56 %. Find:

    a) Mass of water formed.

    b) How many moles of carbon dioxide are obtained?

280 In a receptacle we have 18 g of chloric acid that react with an excess of lithium hydroxide according the following equation:

$$HClO_3 + LiOH \rightarrow LiClO_3 + H_2O$$

The percent yield of the reaction is 52 %. Find:

    a) Mass of water obtained.

    b) How many moles of lithium chlorate are formed?

281 In a flask we have 2.2 mol of hydrogen that react with an excess of nitrogen according the following equation:

$$H_2 + N_2 \rightarrow NH_3 \quad \text{(not balanced)}$$

The percent yield of the reaction is 54 %. Determine:

    a) Mass of ammonia obtained.

    b) How many moles of ammonia are obtained?

282 In a flask we have 7.1 mol of methane that react with an excess of oxygen according the following equation:

$$CH_4 + 2O_2 \rightarrow CO_2 + 2H_2O$$

85.93 L of carbon dioxide gas are obtained at a temperature of 0 °C and a pressure of 1 atm. Determine:

    a) Percent yield of the reaction.

    b) Mass of carbon dioxide obtained.

283 In a balloon flask we have 134.7 L of methane gas at a temperature of 0 °C and a pressure of 1 atm that react with an excess of oxygen according the following equation:

$$CH_4 + 2O_2 \rightarrow CO_2 + 2H_2O$$

The percent yield of the reaction is 47 %. Find:

    a) Mass of water obtained.

    b) How many moles of carbon dioxide are obtained?

284 In a balloon flask we have 168.6 L of ethene gas at a temperature of 248 °C and a pressure of 6.6 atm that react with an excess of oxygen according the following equation:

$C_2H_4 + O_2 \rightarrow CO_2 + H_2O$ (unbalanced)

The percent yield of the reaction is 77 %. Determine:

    a) Mass of water obtained.

    b) How many moles of carbon dioxide are obtained?

285 In a flask we have 6.6 mol of sulfuric acid that react with an excess of zinc according the following equation:

$H_2SO_4 + Zn \rightarrow ZnSO_4 + H_2$

69.53 L of hydrogen gas are obtained at a temperature of 0 °C and a pressure of 1 atm. Calculate:

    a) Percent yield of the reaction.

    b) Mass of hydrogen obtained.

286 In a receptacle we have 39 g of hydrogen that react with an excess of nitrogen according the following equation:

$H_2 + N_2 \rightarrow NH_3$ (unbalanced)

The percent yield of the reaction is 54 %. Find:

    a) Mass of ammonia obtained.

    b) How many moles of ammonia are formed?

287 In a receptacle we have 56 g of ethene that react with an excess of oxygen according the following equation:

$C_2H_4 + 3O_2 \rightarrow 2CO_2 + 2H_2O$

30.34 L of carbon dioxide gas are obtained at a temperature of 35 °C and a pressure of 1.4 atm. Determine:

    a) Percent yield of the reaction.

    b) Mass of carbon dioxide formed.

288 In a receptacle we have 51 g of sulfuric acid that react with an excess of sodium hydroxide according the following equation:

$H_2SO_4 + NaOH \rightarrow Na_2SO_4 + H_2O$ (not balanced)

13.68 g of water are obtained. Find:

    a) Percent yield of the reaction.

    b) Mass of sodium sulfate obtained.

289 In a balloon flask we have 106.3 L of ethene gas at a temperature of 154 °C and a pressure of 2.3 atm that react with an excess of oxygen according the following equation:

$C_2H_4 + 3O_2 \rightarrow 2CO_2 + 2H_2O$

The percent yield of the reaction is 82 %. Calculate:

    a) The volume obtained of carbon dioxide gas at a temperature of 154 °C and a pressure of 2.3 atm.

    b) Mass of water obtained.

290 In a flask we have 7.3 mol of hydrochloric acid that react with an excess of aluminum according the following equation:

$HCl + Al \rightarrow AlCl_3 + H_2$ (not balanced)

14.51 L of hydrogen gas are obtained at a temperature of 120 °C and a pressure of 4.3 atm. Determine:

a) Percent yield of the reaction.

b) Mass of hydrogen formed.

291 In a receptacle we have 34 g of nitrogen that react with an excess of hydrogen according the following equation:

$N_2 + 3H_2 \rightarrow 2NH_3$

28.85 L of ammonia gas are obtained at a temperature of 0 °C and a pressure of 1 atm. Determine:

a) Percent yield of the reaction.

b) Mass of ammonia obtained.

292 In a balloon flask we have 67.3 L of ethene gas at a temperature of 319 °C and a pressure of 3.9 atm that react with an excess of oxygen according the following equation:

$C_2H_4 + O_2 \rightarrow CO_2 + H_2O$ (unbalanced)

97.23 g of water are obtained. Calculate:

a) Percent yield of the reaction.

b) Mass of carbon dioxide obtained.

293 In a balloon flask we have 153.1 L of nitrogen gas at a temperature of 25 °C and a pressure of 1 atm that react with an excess of hydrogen according the following equation:

$N_2 + 3H_2 \rightarrow 2NH_3$

257.2 L of ammonia gas are obtained at a temperature of 25 °C and a pressure of 1 atm. Find:

a) Percent yield of the reaction.

b) Mass of ammonia obtained.

294 In a receptacle we have 430 g of nitrogen that react with an excess of hydrogen according the following equation:

$N_2 + 3H_2 \rightarrow 2NH_3$

The percent yield of the reaction is 65 %. Calculate:

a) Mass of ammonia formed.

b) How many moles of ammonia are obtained?

295 In a receptacle we have 345 g of nitrogen that react with an excess of hydrogen according the following equation:

$N_2 + H_2 \rightarrow NH_3$ (not balanced)

The percent yield of the reaction is 51 %. Determine:

a) The volume obtained of ammonia gas at a temperature of 34 °C and a pressure of 8.6 atm.

b) Mass of ammonia formed.

296 In a receptacle we have 16 g of propane that react with an excess of oxygen according the following equation:

$C_3H_8 + O_2 \rightarrow CO_2 + H_2O$ (unbalanced)

5.904 L of carbon dioxide gas are obtained at a temperature of 157 °C and a pressure of 3 atm. Find:

    a) Percent yield of the reaction.

    b) Mass of carbon dioxide obtained.

297 In a flask we have 1.8 mol of hydrochloric acid that react with an excess of ammonia according the following equation:

$HCl + NH_3 \rightarrow NH_4Cl$

The percent yield of the reaction is 65 %. Determine:

    a) Mass of ammonium chloride obtained.

    b) How many moles of ammonium chloride are formed?

298 In a receptacle we have 83.84 g of aluminum that react with 595 g of hydrochloric acid according the following equation:

$6HCl + 2Al \rightarrow 2AlCl_3 + 3H_2$

Calculate: **a)** The limiting reagent. **b)** Mass of aluminum chloride obtained.

299 In a balloon flask we have 154.1 g of oxygen that react with 166.1 L of hydrogen gas at a temperature of 0 °C and a pressure of 1 atm according the following equation:

$2H_2 + O_2 \rightarrow 2H_2O$

Calculate: **a)** The limiting reagent. **b)** Mass of water obtained.

300 In a flask we have 14.33 g of aluminum hydroxide that react with 79.21 mL of 4.8 mol/L sulfuric acid solution according the following equation:

$3H_2SO_4 + 2Al(OH)_3 \rightarrow Al_2(SO_4)_3 + 6H_2O$

Find: **a)** The limiting reagent. **b)** Mass of aluminum sulfate formed.

301 In a flask we have 2654 mL of 0.8 mol/L calcium hydroxide solution that react with 19530 mL of 0.3 mol/L hydrochloric acid solution according the following equation:

$2HCl + Ca(OH)_2 \rightarrow CaCl_2 + 2H_2O$

Calculate: **a)** The limiting reagent. **b)** Mass of calcium chloride formed.

302 In a receptacle we have 3.78 g of hydrogen that react with 12 g of nitrogen according the following equation:

$N_2 + 3H_2 \rightarrow 2NH_3$

Determine: **a)** The limiting reagent. **b)** Mass of ammonia obtained.

303 In a balloon flask we have 3.874 g of hydrogen that react with 40.07 L of carbon dioxide gas at a temperature of 67 °C and a pressure of 1.7 atm according the following equation:

$CO_2 + H_2 \rightarrow CO + H_2O$

Find: **a)** The limiting reagent. **b)** Mass of water formed.

304 In a flask we have 273.5 g of zinc that react with 1938 mL of 3.8 mol/L sulfuric acid solution according the following equation:

$$H_2SO_4 + Zn \rightarrow ZnSO_4 + H_2$$

Determine: **a)** The limiting reagent. **b)** Mass of zinc sulfate obtained.

305 In a flask we have 480.5 mL of 1.8 mol/L calcium hydroxide solution that react with 488.4 mL of 2.3 mol/L hydrochloric acid solution according the following equation:

$$2HCl + Ca(OH)_2 \rightarrow CaCl_2 + 2H_2O$$

Find: **a)** The limiting reagent. **b)** Mass of water obtained.

306 In a receptacle we have 44.08 g of sodium hydroxide that react with 90.72 g of sulfuric acid according the following equation:

$$H_2SO_4 + 2NaOH \rightarrow Na_2SO_4 + 2H_2O$$

Determine: **a)** The limiting reagent. **b)** Mass of water obtained.

307 In a balloon flask we have 38.65 g of hydrogen that react with 138.3 L of nitrogen gas at a temperature of 101 °C and a pressure of 1 atm according the following equation:

$$N_2 + 3H_2 \rightarrow 2NH_3$$

Calculate: **a)** The limiting reagent. **b)** Mass of ammonia formed.

308 In a flask we have 8.327 g of ammonia that react with 202.7 mL of 1.8 mol/L sulfuric acid solution according the following equation:

$$H_2SO_4 + 2NH_3 \rightarrow (NH_4)_2SO_4$$

Determine: **a)** The limiting reagent. **b)** Mass of ammonium sulfate obtained.

309 In a flask we have 1775 mL of 0.3 mol/L lithium hydroxide solution that react with 1198 mL of 0.8 mol/L chloric acid solution according the following equation:

$$HClO_3 + LiOH \rightarrow LiClO_3 + H_2O$$

Calculate: **a)** The limiting reagent. **b)** Mass of water obtained.

310 In a receptacle we have 955.4 g of hydrogen chloride that react with 783.2 g of ammonia according the following equation:

$$NH_3 + HCl \rightarrow NH_4Cl$$

Determine: **a)** The limiting reagent. **b)** Mass of ammonium chloride formed.

311 In a balloon flask we have 87.11 g of oxygen that react with 29.08 L of ethene gas at a temperature of 25 °C and a pressure of 1 atm according the following equation:

$$C_2H_4 + 3O_2 \rightarrow 2CO_2 + 2H_2O$$

Determine: **a)** The limiting reagent. **b)** Mass of carbon dioxide formed.

312 In a flask we have 432.3 g of aluminum hydroxide that react with 10450 mL of 0.8 mol/L hydrochloric acid solution according the following equation:

$$3HCl + Al(OH)_3 \rightarrow AlCl_3 + 3H_2O$$

Find: **a)** The limiting reagent. **b)** Mass of aluminum chloride formed.

313 In a flask we have 175 mL of 3.8 mol/L aluminum hydroxide solution that react with 1781 mL of 0.8 mol/L hydrochloric acid solution according the following equation:

$3HCl + Al(OH)_3 \rightarrow AlCl_3 + 3H_2O$

Determine: **a)** The limiting reagent. **b)** Mass of aluminum chloride obtained.

314 In a flask we have 27.76 g of sodium hydroxide that react with 174.4 mL of 3.8 mol/L sulfuric acid solution according the following equation:

$H_2SO_4 + 2NaOH \rightarrow Na_2SO_4 + 2H_2O$

Calculate: **a)** The limiting reagent. **b)** Mass of water obtained.

315 In a balloon flask we have 61.69 g of nitrogen that react with 100.1 L of hydrogen gas at a temperature of 0 °C and a pressure of 1 atm according the following equation:

$3H_2 + N_2 \rightarrow 2NH_3$

Find: **a)** The limiting reagent. **b)** Mass of ammonia obtained.

316 In a flask we have 41.76 g of ammonia that react with 479.5 mL of 2.8 mol/L hydrochloric acid solution according the following equation:

$HCl + NH_3 \rightarrow NH_4Cl$

Find: **a)** The limiting reagent. **b)** Mass of ammonium chloride formed.

317 In a flask we have 97.6 mL of 2.3 mol/L aluminum hydroxide solution that react with 396.3 mL of 1.3 mol/L sulfuric acid solution according the following equation:

$3H_2SO_4 + 2Al(OH)_3 \rightarrow Al_2(SO_4)_3 + 6H_2O$

Calculate: **a)** The limiting reagent. **b)** Mass of aluminum sulfate obtained.

318 In a receptacle we have 174.9 g of hydrogen chloride that react with 45 g of ammonia according the following equation:

$NH_3 + HCl \rightarrow NH_4Cl$

Calculate: **a)** The limiting reagent. **b)** Mass of ammonium chloride obtained.

319 In a balloon flask we have 90.43 g of hydrogen that react with 189.1 L of nitrogen gas at a temperature of 25 °C and a pressure of 1 atm according the following equation:

$N_2 + 3H_2 \rightarrow 2NH_3$

Find: **a)** The limiting reagent. **b)** Mass of ammonia obtained.

320 In a flask we have 19.52 g of lithium hydroxide that react with 200.7 mL of 2.3 mol/L chloric acid solution according the following equation:

$HClO_3 + LiOH \rightarrow LiClO_3 + H_2O$

Find: **a)** The limiting reagent. **b)** Mass of lithium chlorate obtained.

321 In a balloon flask we have 110.4 g of nitrogen that react with 22.5 L of hydrogen gas at a temperature of 25 °C and a pressure of 9.6 atm according the following equation:

$3H_2 + N_2 \rightarrow 2NH_3$

Calculate: **a)** The limiting reagent. **b)** Mass of ammonia obtained.

322 In a receptacle we have 185.8 g of ammonia that react with 425 g of sulfuric acid according the following equation:

$$H_2SO_4 + 2NH_3 \rightarrow (NH_4)_2SO_4$$

Find: **a)** The limiting reagent. **b)** Mass of ammonium sulfate obtained.

323 In a balloon flask we have 51.86 g of nitrogen that react with 131.8 L of hydrogen gas at a temperature of 172 °C and a pressure of 1 atm according the following equation:

$$3H_2 + N_2 \rightarrow 2NH_3$$

Determine: **a)** The limiting reagent. **b)** Mass of ammonia formed.

324 In a flask we have 443.8 g of sodium hydroxide that react with 11900 mL of 1.8 mol/L hydrochloric acid solution according the following equation:

$$HCl + NaOH \rightarrow NaCl + H_2O$$

Calculate: **a)** The limiting reagent. **b)** Mass of sodium chloride formed.

325 In a balloon flask we have 12.38 g of oxygen that react with 2.2 L of methane gas at a temperature of 0 °C and a pressure of 1 atm according the following equation:

$$CH_4 + 2O_2 \rightarrow CO_2 + 2H_2O$$

Find: **a)** The limiting reagent. **b)** Mass of carbon dioxide obtained.

326 In a balloon flask we have 5.006 g of hydrogen that react with 110 L of carbon dioxide gas at a temperature of 0 °C and a pressure of 1 atm according the following equation:

$$CO_2 + H_2 \rightarrow CO + H_2O$$

Determine: **a)** The limiting reagent. **b)** Mass of carbon monoxide formed.

327 In a balloon flask we have 76.04 g of nitrogen that react with 261.1 L of hydrogen gas at a temperature of 0 °C and a pressure of 1 atm according the following equation:

$$3H_2 + N_2 \rightarrow 2NH_3$$

Find: **a)** The limiting reagent. **b)** Mass of ammonia obtained.

328 In a flask we have 52.63 g of aluminum hydroxide that react with 135.3 mL of 4.3 mol/L sulfuric acid solution according the following equation:

$$3H_2SO_4 + 2Al(OH)_3 \rightarrow Al_2(SO_4)_3 + 6H_2O$$

Determine: **a)** The limiting reagent. **b)** Mass of aluminum sulfate obtained.

329 In a flask we have 54.22 mL of 4.8 mol/L calcium hydroxide solution that react with 241.3 mL of 3.3 mol/L hydrochloric acid solution according the following equation:

$$2HCl + Ca(OH)_2 \rightarrow CaCl_2 + 2H_2O$$

Determine: **a)** The limiting reagent. **b)** Mass of water obtained.

330 In a balloon flask we have 38.03 g of nitrogen that react with 96.8 L of hydrogen gas at a temperature of 248 °C and a pressure of 1 atm according the following equation:

$$3H_2 + N_2 \rightarrow 2NH_3$$

Find: **a)** The limiting reagent. **b)** Mass of ammonia formed.

331 In a balloon flask we have 7.495 g of nitrogen that react with 23.58 L of hydrogen gas at a temperature of 0 °C and a pressure of 1 atm according the following equation:

$$3H_2 + N_2 \rightarrow 2NH_3$$

Find: **a)** The limiting reagent. **b)** Mass of ammonia formed.

332 In a flask we have 20.63 g of zinc that react with 129.8 mL of 3.8 mol/L hydrochloric acid solution according the following equation:

$$2HCl + Zn \rightarrow ZnCl_2 + H_2$$

Find: **a)** The limiting reagent. **b)** Mass of hydrogen formed.

333 In a flask we have 47.65 mL of 2.3 mol/L calcium hydroxide solution that react with 84.35 mL of 3.3 mol/L hydrochloric acid solution according the following equation:

$$2HCl + Ca(OH)_2 \rightarrow CaCl_2 + 2H_2O$$

Calculate: **a)** The limiting reagent. **b)** Mass of calcium chloride obtained.

334 In a flask we have 28.93 g of sodium hydroxide that react with 304.4 mL of 1.8 mol/L hydrochloric acid solution according the following equation:

$$HCl + NaOH \rightarrow NaCl + H_2O$$

Determine: **a)** The limiting reagent. **b)** Mass of water formed.

335 In a balloon flask we have 13.28 g of hydrogen that react with 96.7 L of carbon dioxide gas at a temperature of 25 °C and a pressure of 1 atm according the following equation:

$$CO_2 + H_2 \rightarrow CO + H_2O$$

Calculate: **a)** The limiting reagent. **b)** Mass of water obtained.

336 In a flask we have 33.45 g of calcium hydroxide that react with 498.6 mL of 3.3 mol/L hydrochloric acid solution according the following equation:

$$2HCl + Ca(OH)_2 \rightarrow CaCl_2 + 2H_2O$$

Calculate: **a)** The limiting reagent. **b)** Mass of calcium chloride formed.

337 In a flask we have 130.5 mL of 2.8 mol/L aluminum hydroxide solution that react with 2055 mL of 0.8 mol/L hydrochloric acid solution according the following equation:

$$3HCl + Al(OH)_3 \rightarrow AlCl_3 + 3H_2O$$

Determine: **a)** The limiting reagent. **b)** Mass of aluminum chloride obtained.

338 In a receptacle we have 154.3 g of oxygen that react with 84.15 g of ethene according the following equation:

$$C_2H_4 + 3O_2 \rightarrow 2CO_2 + 2H_2O$$

Determine: **a)** The limiting reagent. **b)** Mass of water formed.

339 In a balloon flask we have 19.88 g of hydrogen that react with 218.9 L of carbon dioxide gas at a temperature of 25 °C and a pressure of 2 atm according the following equation:

$$CO_2 + H_2 \rightarrow CO + H_2O$$

Determine: **a)** The limiting reagent. **b)** Mass of water obtained.

340 In a flask we have 275 g of carbon dioxide that react with 9327 mL of 1.3 mol/L sodium hydroxide solution according the following equation:

$$NaOH + CO_2 \rightarrow NaHCO_3$$

Find: **a)** The limiting reagent. **b)** Mass of sodium bicarbonate obtained.

341 In a flask we have 121.1 mL of 4.3 mol/L sodium hydroxide solution that react with 310.1 mL of 2.3 mol/L hydrochloric acid solution according the following equation:

$$HCl + NaOH \rightarrow NaCl + H_2O$$

Calculate: **a)** The limiting reagent. **b)** Mass of water formed.

342 In a receptacle we have 47.24 g of hydrogen chloride that react with 32.56 g of ammonia according the following equation:

$$NH_3 + HCl \rightarrow NH_4Cl$$

Determine: **a)** The limiting reagent. **b)** Mass of ammonium chloride formed.

343 In a balloon flask we have 47.35 g of hydrogen that react with 316.7 L of nitrogen gas at a temperature of 0 °C and a pressure of 1 atm according the following equation:

$$N_2 + 3H_2 \rightarrow 2NH_3$$

Find: **a)** The limiting reagent. **b)** Mass of ammonia formed.

344 In a flask we have 11.98 g of ammonia that react with 59.08 mL of 3.8 mol/L sulfuric acid solution according the following equation:

$$H_2SO_4 + 2NH_3 \rightarrow (NH_4)_2SO_4$$

Calculate: **a)** The limiting reagent. **b)** Mass of ammonium sulfate obtained.

345 In a flask we have 708.4 mL of 1.8 mol/L ammonia solution that react with 254.4 mL of 2.8 mol/L hydrochloric acid solution according the following equation:

$$HCl + NH_3 \rightarrow NH_4Cl$$

Calculate: **a)** The limiting reagent. **b)** Mass of ammonium chloride formed.

346 In a flask we have 223.6 mL of 4.8 mol/L lithium hydroxide solution that react with 427.9 mL of 1.3 mol/L chloric acid solution according the following equation:

$$HClO_3 + LiOH \rightarrow LiClO_3 + H_2O$$

Calculate: **a)** The limiting reagent. **b)** Mass of water obtained.

347 In a balloon flask we have 1312 g of oxygen that react with 294.7 L of propane gas at a temperature of 25 °C and a pressure of 1.3 atm according the following equation:

$$C_3H_8 + 5O_2 \rightarrow 3CO_2 + 4H_2O$$

Calculate: **a)** The limiting reagent. **b)** Mass of water formed.

348 In a flask we have 17.04 g of aluminum hydroxide that react with 74.2 mL of 4.8 mol/L hydrochloric acid solution according the following equation:

$$3HCl + Al(OH)_3 \rightarrow AlCl_3 + 3H_2O$$

Calculate: **a)** The limiting reagent. **b)** Mass of water formed.

349 In a flask we have 1458 mL of 2.8 mol/L lithium hydroxide solution that react with 3462 mL of 2.3 mol/L chloric acid solution according the following equation:

$$HClO_3 + LiOH \rightarrow LiClO_3 + H_2O$$

Determine: **a)** The limiting reagent. **b)** Mass of water obtained.

350 In a receptacle we have 34.9 g of aluminum hydroxide that react with 61.74 g of hydrochloric acid according the following equation:

$$3HCl + Al(OH)_3 \rightarrow AlCl_3 + 3H_2O$$

Determine: **a)** The limiting reagent. **b)** Mass of aluminum chloride formed.

351 In a flask we have 58.97 g of sodium hydroxide that react with 129.9 mL of 3.3 mol/L sulfuric acid solution according the following equation:

$$H_2SO_4 + 2NaOH \rightarrow Na_2SO_4 + 2H_2O$$

Find: **a)** The limiting reagent. **b)** Mass of water obtained.

352 In a balloon flask we have 920.9 g of oxygen that react with 254.1 L of propane gas at a temperature of 0 °C and a pressure of 1 atm according the following equation:

$$C_3H_8 + 5O_2 \rightarrow 3CO_2 + 4H_2O$$

Calculate: **a)** The limiting reagent. **b)** Mass of water formed.

353 In a flask we have 1301 mL of 0.8 mol/L ammonia solution that react with 587.5 mL of 2.8 mol/L hydrochloric acid solution according the following equation:

$$HCl + NH_3 \rightarrow NH_4Cl$$

Calculate: **a)** The limiting reagent. **b)** Mass of ammonium chloride formed.

354 In a receptacle we have 96 g of oxygen that react with 47.52 g of methane according the following equation:

$$CH_4 + 2O_2 \rightarrow CO_2 + 2H_2O$$

Calculate: **a)** The limiting reagent. **b)** Mass of carbon dioxide obtained.

355 In a balloon flask we have 1219 g of oxygen that react with 121.2 L of ethene gas at a temperature of 25 °C and a pressure of 5.1 atm according the following equation:

$$C_2H_4 + 3O_2 \rightarrow 2CO_2 + 2H_2O$$

Calculate: **a)** The limiting reagent. **b)** Mass of carbon dioxide formed.

356 In a flask we have 27.02 g of zinc that react with 126.9 mL of 2.8 mol/L phosphoric acid solution according the following equation:

$$2H_3PO_4 + 3Zn \rightarrow Zn_3(PO_4)_2 + 3H_2$$

Determine: **a)** The limiting reagent. **b)** Mass of zinc phosphate obtained.

357 In a balloon flask we have 25.83 g of oxygen that react with 14.9 L of hydrogen gas at a temperature of 328 °C and a pressure of 3.2 atm according the following equation:

$$2H_2 + O_2 \rightarrow 2H_2O$$

Determine: **a)** The limiting reagent. **b)** Mass of water formed.

358 In a balloon flask we have 199 g of oxygen that react with 117.9 L of ethene gas at a temperature of 25 °C and a pressure of 0.8 atm according the following equation:

$C_2H_4 + 3O_2 \rightarrow 2CO_2 + 2H_2O$

Calculate: **a)** The limiting reagent. **b)** Mass of carbon dioxide obtained.

359 In a balloon flask we have 139.6 g of oxygen that react with 66.99 L of methane gas at a temperature of 0 °C and a pressure of 1 atm according the following equation:

$CH_4 + 2O_2 \rightarrow CO_2 + 2H_2O$

Calculate: **a)** The limiting reagent. **b)** Mass of carbon dioxide formed.

360 In a flask we have 15.92 g of sodium hydroxide that react with 85.03 mL of 1.8 mol/L sulfuric acid solution according the following equation:

$H_2SO_4 + 2NaOH \rightarrow Na_2SO_4 + 2H_2O$

Find: **a)** The limiting reagent. **b)** Mass of water formed.

361 In a flask we have 264 mL of 1.3 mol/L lithium hydroxide solution that react with 823.7 mL of 0.8 mol/L chloric acid solution according the following equation:

$HClO_3 + LiOH \rightarrow LiClO_3 + H_2O$

Find: **a)** The limiting reagent. **b)** Mass of water formed.

362 In a receptacle we have 67.72 g of sodium hydroxide that react with 37 g of hydrochloric acid according the following equation:

$HCl + NaOH \rightarrow NaCl + H_2O$

Find: **a)** The limiting reagent. **b)** Mass of sodium chloride obtained.

363 In a balloon flask we have 320.5 g of nitrogen that react with 142.2 L of hydrogen gas at a temperature of 43 °C and a pressure of 3.6 atm according the following equation:

$3H_2 + N_2 \rightarrow 2NH_3$

Calculate: **a)** The limiting reagent. **b)** Mass of ammonia obtained.

364 In a flask we have 512 g of carbon dioxide that react with 2652 mL of 3.3 mol/L sodium hydroxide solution according the following equation:

$NaOH + CO_2 \rightarrow NaHCO_3$

Determine: **a)** The limiting reagent. **b)** Mass of sodium bicarbonate obtained.

365 In a flask we have 214.1 mL of 4.3 mol/L potassium hydroxide solution that react with 407 mL of 3.8 mol/L nitric acid solution according the following equation:

$HNO_3 + KOH \rightarrow KNO_3 + H_2O$

Determine: **a)** The limiting reagent. **b)** Mass of potassium nitrate formed.

366 In a receptacle we have 45.62 g of calcium hydroxide that react with 64.35 g of hydrochloric acid according the following equation:

$2HCl + Ca(OH)_2 \rightarrow CaCl_2 + 2H_2O$

Determine: **a)** The limiting reagent. **b)** Mass of water formed.

367 In a balloon flask we have 98.51 g of nitrogen that react with 171 L of hydrogen gas at a temperature of 25 °C and a pressure of 1 atm according the following equation:

$3H_2 + N_2 \rightarrow 2NH_3$

Find: **a)** The limiting reagent. **b)** Mass of ammonia obtained.

368 In a flask we have 26.47 g of lithium hydroxide that react with 207.1 mL of 2.8 mol/L chloric acid solution according the following equation:

$HClO_3 + LiOH \rightarrow LiClO_3 + H_2O$

Find: **a)** The limiting reagent. **b)** Mass of lithium chlorate formed.

369 In a flask we have 432.9 mL of 3.3 mol/L aluminum hydroxide solution that react with 1301 mL of 2.8 mol/L sulfuric acid solution according the following equation:

$3H_2SO_4 + 2Al(OH)_3 \rightarrow Al_2(SO_4)_3 + 6H_2O$

Calculate: **a)** The limiting reagent. **b)** Mass of aluminum sulfate formed.

370 In a receptacle we have 1282 g of hydrogen chloride that react with 300 g of ammonia according the following equation:

$NH_3 + HCl \rightarrow NH_4Cl$

Determine: **a)** The limiting reagent. **b)** Mass of ammonium chloride obtained.

371 In a balloon flask we have 22.13 g of oxygen that react with 4.805 L of propane gas at a temperature of 0 °C and a pressure of 1 atm according the following equation:

$C_3H_8 + 5O_2 \rightarrow 3CO_2 + 4H_2O$

Calculate: **a)** The limiting reagent. **b)** Mass of carbon dioxide obtained.

372 In a flask we have 72.55 g of aluminum that react with 4255 mL of 1.8 mol/L sulfuric acid solution according the following equation:

$3H_2SO_4 + 2Al \rightarrow Al_2(SO_4)_3 + 3H_2$

Determine: **a)** The limiting reagent. **b)** Mass of hydrogen formed.

373 In a flask we have 42.58 g of calcium hydroxide that react with 402.7 mL of 4.8 mol/L hydrochloric acid solution according the following equation:

$2HCl + Ca(OH)_2 \rightarrow CaCl_2 + 2H_2O$

Find: **a)** The limiting reagent. **b)** Mass of calcium chloride formed.

374 In a receptacle we have 20.49 g of ammonia that react with 62.48 g of hydrochloric acid according the following equation:

$HCl + NH_3 \rightarrow NH_4Cl$

Calculate: **a)** The limiting reagent. **b)** Mass of ammonium chloride formed.

375 In a balloon flask we have 428.4 g of oxygen that react with 90.9 L of ethene gas at a temperature of 62 °C and a pressure of 1 atm according the following equation:

$C_2H_4 + 3O_2 \rightarrow 2CO_2 + 2H_2O$

Calculate: **a)** The limiting reagent. **b)** Mass of carbon dioxide formed.

376 In a flask we have 310.7 g of sodium hydroxide that react with 4426 mL of 1.3 mol/L hydrochloric acid solution according the following equation:

$$HCl + NaOH \rightarrow NaCl + H_2O$$

Determine: **a)** The limiting reagent. **b)** Mass of sodium chloride formed.

377 In a flask we have 1048 mL of 1.8 mol/L ammonia solution that react with 286.7 mL of 4.3 mol/L hydrochloric acid solution according the following equation:

$$HCl + NH_3 \rightarrow NH_4Cl$$

Calculate: **a)** The limiting reagent. **b)** Mass of ammonium chloride formed.

378 In a flask we have 42.09 g of zinc that react with 1268 mL of 1.3 mol/L hydrochloric acid solution according the following equation:

$$2HCl + Zn \rightarrow ZnCl_2 + H_2$$

Determine: **a)** The limiting reagent. **b)** Mass of zinc chloride formed.

379 In a balloon flask we have 5.568 g of nitrogen that react with 8.2 L of hydrogen gas at a temperature of 25 °C and a pressure of 1 atm according the following equation:

$$3H_2 + N_2 \rightarrow 2NH_3$$

Determine: **a)** The limiting reagent. **b)** Mass of ammonia formed.

380 In a flask we have 7.714 g of aluminum that react with 116.9 mL of 4.3 mol/L phosphoric acid solution according the following equation:

$$2H_3PO_4 + 2Al \rightarrow 2AlPO_4 + 3H_2$$

Find: **a)** The limiting reagent. **b)** Mass of aluminum phosphate obtained.

381 In a flask we have 797.6 mL of 2.8 mol/L ammonia solution that react with 325.3 mL of 4.8 mol/L hydrochloric acid solution according the following equation:

$$HCl + NH_3 \rightarrow NH_4Cl$$

Find: **a)** The limiting reagent. **b)** Mass of ammonium chloride formed.

382 In a receptacle we have 40.3 g of zinc that react with 60.75 g of hydrochloric acid according the following equation:

$$2HCl + Zn \rightarrow ZnCl_2 + H_2$$

Determine: **a)** The limiting reagent. **b)** Mass of hydrogen obtained.

383 In a balloon flask we have 25.7 g of hydrogen that react with 59.9 L of carbon dioxide gas at a temperature of 25 °C and a pressure of 2.9 atm according the following equation:

$$CO_2 + H_2 \rightarrow CO + H_2O$$

Find: **a)** The limiting reagent. **b)** Mass of carbon monoxide obtained.

384 In a flask we have 32.57 g of aluminum hydroxide that react with 1233 mL of 0.8 mol/L hydrochloric acid solution according the following equation:

$$3HCl + Al(OH)_3 \rightarrow AlCl_3 + 3H_2O$$

Find: **a)** The limiting reagent. **b)** Mass of aluminum chloride formed.

385 In a flask we have 2862 mL of 3.8 mol/L calcium hydroxide solution that react with 6393 mL of 1.8 mol/L hydrochloric acid solution according the following equation:

$2HCl + Ca(OH)_2 \rightarrow CaCl_2 + 2H_2O$

Calculate: **a)** The limiting reagent. **b)** Mass of water formed.

386 In a receptacle we have 16.38 g of aluminum hydroxide that react with 34.5 g of hydrochloric acid according the following equation:

$3HCl + Al(OH)_3 \rightarrow AlCl_3 + 3H_2O$

Calculate: **a)** The limiting reagent. **b)** Mass of water obtained.

387 In a balloon flask we have 7.321 g of hydrogen that react with 195.1 L of carbon dioxide gas at a temperature of 160 °C and a pressure of 1 atm according the following equation:

$CO_2 + H_2 \rightarrow CO + H_2O$

Calculate: **a)** The limiting reagent. **b)** Mass of carbon monoxide formed.

388 In a flask we have 46.53 g of sodium hydroxide that react with 1287 mL of 0.8 mol/L sulfuric acid solution according the following equation:

$H_2SO_4 + 2NaOH \rightarrow Na_2SO_4 + 2H_2O$

Determine: **a)** The limiting reagent. **b)** Mass of sodium sulfate obtained.

389 In a flask we have 128.5 mL of 1.8 mol/L aluminum hydroxide solution that react with 329.6 mL of 1.8 mol/L sulfuric acid solution according the following equation:

$3H_2SO_4 + 2Al(OH)_3 \rightarrow Al_2(SO_4)_3 + 6H_2O$

Determine: **a)** The limiting reagent. **b)** Mass of water formed.

390 In a receptacle we have 47.3 g of sodium hydroxide that react with 26 g of hydrochloric acid according the following equation:

$HCl + NaOH \rightarrow NaCl + H_2O$

Determine: **a)** The limiting reagent. **b)** Mass of sodium chloride formed.

391 In a balloon flask we have 129 g of oxygen that react with 116.6 L of methane gas at a temperature of 100 °C and a pressure of 1 atm according the following equation:

$CH_4 + 2O_2 \rightarrow CO_2 + 2H_2O$

Determine: **a)** The limiting reagent. **b)** Mass of water obtained.

392 In a flask we have 58.79 g of calcium hydroxide that react with 8846 mL of 0.3 mol/L hydrochloric acid solution according the following equation:

$2HCl + Ca(OH)_2 \rightarrow CaCl_2 + 2H_2O$

Determine: **a)** The limiting reagent. **b)** Mass of calcium chloride obtained.

393 In a flask we have 116.2 mL of 3.3 mol/L sodium hydroxide solution that react with 364.4 mL of 1.8 mol/L hydrochloric acid solution according the following equation:

$HCl + NaOH \rightarrow NaCl + H_2O$

Find: **a)** The limiting reagent. **b)** Mass of water obtained.

394 In a receptacle we have 156.4 g of oxygen that react with 73.1 g of propane according the following equation:

$$C_3H_8 + 5O_2 \rightarrow 3CO_2 + 4H_2O$$

Calculate: **a)** The limiting reagent. **b)** Mass of water formed.

395 In a balloon flask we have 7326 g of oxygen that react with 195.7 L of propane gas at a temperature of 25 °C and a pressure of 9.1 atm according the following equation:

$$C_3H_8 + 5O_2 \rightarrow 3CO_2 + 4H_2O$$

Determine: **a)** The limiting reagent. **b)** Mass of carbon dioxide obtained.

396 In a flask we have 2.755 g of aluminum that react with 111.5 mL of 1.3 mol/L phosphoric acid solution according the following equation:

$$2H_3PO_4 + 2Al \rightarrow 2AlPO_4 + 3H_2$$

Find: **a)** The limiting reagent. **b)** Mass of hydrogen obtained.

Solutions

Answers:

1	**a)** 88.05 L, **b)** 70.71 g.
2	**a)** 6.9 mol, **b)** 6.9 mol.
3	**a)** 6 mol, **b)** 12 mol.
4	**a)** 305.7 L, **b)** 360 g.
5	**a)** 1744 mL, **b)** 135 g.
6	**a)** 160.7 L, **b)** 186.1 g.
7	**a)** 0.6925 L, **b)** 23.05 g.
8	**a)** 112.1 L, **b)** 180 g.
9	**a)** 141.6 g, **b)** 2.647 mol.
10	**a)** 65.09 L, **b)** 191.5 g.
11	**a)** 485 mL, **b)** 88.26 g.
12	**a)** 125.2 g, **b)** 1.385 mol.
13	**a)** 1.81 L, **b)** 84.04 g.
14	**a)** 2051 mL, **b)** 11.08 g.
15	**a)** 3.5 mol, **b)** 3.5 mol.
16	**a)** 1722 g, **b)** 71.76 mol.
17	**a)** 1303 mL, **b)** 191.3 g.
18	**a)** 146.5 L, **b)** 6.536 mol.
19	**a)** 166.9 L, **b)** 134 g.
20	**a)** 10230 mL, **b)** 5804 g.
21	**a)** 49 g, **b)** 0.6712 mol.
22	**a)** 250.7 L, **b)** 190.1 g.
23	**a)** 137 mL, **b)** 44.73 g.
24	**a)** 97.53 g, **b)** 1.096 mol.
25	**a)** 11.32 L, **b)** 4.124 g.
26	**a)** 120.8 mL, **b)** 1.378 g.
27	**a)** 8.7 mol, **b)** 8.7 mol.
28	**a)** 275.7 L, **b)** 295.2 g.
29	**a)** 4778 mL, **b)** 1135 g.
30	**a)** 3.43 g, **b)** 0.09528 mol.
31	**a)** 123.9 L, **b)** 99.5 g.
32	**a)** 1443 mL, **b)** 400.1 g.
33	**a)** 5.686 L, **b)** 80.77 g.
34	**a)** 11.53 L, **b)** 38.34 g.
35	**a)** 104.4 mL, **b)** 4.886 g.
36	**a)** 31 g, **b)** 10.33 mol.
37	**a)** 7.722 L, **b)** 28.09 g.
38	**a)** 102 mL, **b)** 38.39 g.
39	**a)** 0.4 mol, **b)** 0.4 mol.
40	**a)** 80.74 L, **b)** 424.7 g.
41	**a)** 1462 mL, **b)** 5.7 g.
42	**a)** 68.7 L, **b)** 31.36 mol.
43	**a)** 82.57 mL, **b)** 0.355 mol.
44	**a)** 1701 mL, **b)** 72.45 g.

45	a) 10720 mL,	b) 1171 g.
46	a) 1.171 L,	b) 18.03 g.
47	a) 1138 mL,	b) 65.84 g.
48	a) 420 g,	b) 3.107 mol.
49	a) 2026 mL,	b) 175.1 g.
50	a) 139.1 mL,	b) 1.378 g.
51	a) 12.22 L,	b) 82.48 g.
52	a) 82.93 L,	b) 329.3 g.
53	a) 3250 mL,	b) 7.8 g.
54	a) 267.6 mL,	b) 51.21 g.
55	a) 477.3 L,	b) 3459 g.
56	a) 1299 mL,	b) 264.2 g.
57	a) 47.38 mL,	b) 0.199 mol.
58	a) 8.778 L,	b) 16.22 g.
59	a) 79.31 mL,	b) 5.425 g.
60	a) 15 g,	b) 0.2296 mol.
61	a) 87.58 L,	b) 31.33 g.
62	a) 488.4 mL,	b) 65.71 g.
63	a) 2 mol,	b) 3 mol.
64	a) 5.399 L,	b) 81.82 g.
65	a) 2000 mL,	b) 227.2 g.
66	a) 41.2 L,	b) 5.95 mol.
67	a) 137.8 L,	b) 875.9 g.
68	a) 819.5 mL,	b) 166.6 g.
69	a) 684.9 mL,	b) 0.1826 mol.
70	a) 6.861 L,	b) 24.9 g.
71	a) 1266 mL,	b) 59.24 g.
72	a) 24 g,	b) 1.714 mol.
73	a) 86.96 mL,	b) 0.2 g.
74	a) 369.4 mL,	b) 84.97 g.
75	a) 190.8 g,	b) 1.767 mol.
76	a) 118.9 L,	b) 419.6 g.
77	a) 1349 mL,	b) 339.3 g.
78	a) 118.2 mL,	b) 0.449 mol.
79	a) 549.3 L,	b) 880.9 g.
80	a) 21300 mL,	b) 1431 g.
81	a) 65.38 g,	b) 0.4795 mol.
82	a) 0.7073 L,	b) 30.79 g.
83	a) 221.4 mL,	b) 32.82 g.
84	a) 44.42 mL,	b) 4.478 g.
85	a) 87.11 L,	b) 93.27 g.
86	a) 215.3 mL,	b) 32.25 g.
87	a) 187.2 g,	b) 1.733 mol.
88	a) 810.7 L,	b) 489.6 g.
89	a) 1953 mL,	b) 449.4 g.

90	**a)** 193.8 L, **b)** 3.666 mol.
91	**a)** 0.5 mol, **b)** 0.5 mol.
92	**a)** 3231 mL, **b)** 4.2 g.
93	**a)** 10.29 g, **b)** 0.09524 mol.
94	**a)** 102.5 L, **b)** 71.25 g.
95	**a)** 340.9 mL, **b)** 43.52 g.
96	**a)** 270 g, **b)** 4.117 mol.
97	**a)** 1.429 L, **b)** 75.66 g.
98	**a)** 364.8 mL, **b)** 11.82 g.
99	**a)** 7.8 mol, **b)** 3.9 mol.

100 **a)** $H_4P_2O_7 + 4AgBr \rightarrow 4HBr + Ag_4P_2O_7$
b) 257.43 g, 1.371 mol, **c)** 207.54 g, 0.3427 mol.

101 **a)** $MgO + Cd(NO_3)_2 \rightarrow Mg(NO_3)_2 + CdO$
b) 310.9 g, 1.315 mol, **c)** 168.86 g, 1.315 mol.

102 **a)** $3ZnCO_3 + 2FeCl_3 \rightarrow 3ZnCl_2 + Fe_2(CO_3)_3$
b) 33.65 g, 0.2073 mol, **c)** 30.23 g, 0.1037 mol.

103 **a)** $3H_2SO_4 + 2Fe(NO_3)_3 \rightarrow 6HNO_3 + Fe_2(SO_4)_3$
b) 78.96 g, 0.3265 mol, **c)** 65.24 g, 0.1633 mol.

104 **a)** $MgCl_2 + Li_2SO_4 \rightarrow MgSO_4 + 2LiCl$
b) 81.8 g, 0.745 mol, **c)** 63.18 g, 1.49 mol.

105 **a)** $2MgS + Pb(CO_3)_2 \rightarrow 2MgCO_3 + PbS_2$
b) 273.15 g, 0.8348 mol, **c)** 226.4 g, 0.8348 mol.

106 **a)** $Al_2S_3 + 3H_2CO_3 \rightarrow Al_2(CO_3)_3 + 3H_2S$
b) 100.44 g, 1.62 mol, **c)** 55.08 g, 1.62 mol.

107 **a)** $2FeBr_3 + 3CaCO_3 \rightarrow Fe_2(CO_3)_3 + 3CaBr_2$
b) 48.78 g, 0.4873 mol, **c)** 97.41 g, 0.4873 mol.

108 **a)** $Fe(ClO)_3 + 3NaClO_3 \rightarrow Fe(ClO_3)_3 + 3NaClO$
b) 72.92 g, 0.6847 mol, **c)** 51.01 g, 0.6847 mol.

109 **a)** $Ca(NO_3)_2 + CuO \rightarrow CaO + Cu(NO_3)_2$
b) 13.56 g, 0.1706 mol, **c)** 31.99 g, 0.1706 mol.

110 **a)** $2Zn(OH)_2 + PbO_2 \rightarrow 2ZnO + Pb(OH)_4$
b) 91.44 g, 0.3823 mol, **c)** 105.21 g, 0.3823 mol.

111 **a)** $3PbCl_4 + 4Fe(NO_3)_3 \rightarrow 3Pb(NO_3)_4 + 4FeCl_3$
b) 90.48 g, 0.3742 mol, **c)** 60.73 g, 0.3742 mol.

112 **a)** $Mg_2P_2O_7 + 4KCl \rightarrow 2MgCl_2 + K_4P_2O_7$
b) 117.97 g, 1.581 mol, **c)** 130.62 g, 0.3953 mol.

113 **a)** $2Li_2SO_4 + Pb(OH)_4 \rightarrow 4LiOH + Pb(SO_4)_2$
b) 26.32 g, 0.0956 mol, **c)** 38.17 g, 0.0956 mol.

114 **a)** $Ag_2O + K_2CO_3 \rightarrow Ag_2CO_3 + K_2O$
b) 17.89 g, 0.1294 mol, **c)** 12.19 g, 0.1294 mol.

115 **a)** $2MgCO_3 + K_4P_2O_7 \rightarrow Mg_2P_2O_7 + 2K_2CO_3$
b) 66.63 g, 0.2017 mol, **c)** 55.74 g, 0.4033 mol.

116 **a)** $2Cu_2SO_4 + Mg_2P_2O_7 \rightarrow Cu_4P_2O_7 + 2MgSO_4$
b) 46.42 g, 0.2085 mol, **c)** 50.17 g, 0.417 mol.

117   **a)** $3H_2SO_4 + Cr_2S_3 \rightarrow 3H_2S + Cr_2(SO_4)_3$

      b) 46.94 g, 0.2347 mol,   **c)** 92 g, 0.2347 mol.

118   **a)** $6HNO_3 + Al_2O_3 \rightarrow 3H_2O + 2Al(NO_3)_3$

      b) 25.37 g, 0.2487 mol,   **c)** 105.94 g, 0.4974 mol.

119   **a)** $MgCl_2 + 2HClO \rightarrow Mg(ClO)_2 + 2HCl$

      b) 23.14 g, 0.4407 mol,   **c)** 16.09 g, 0.4407 mol.

120   **a)** $2HCl + Mg(OH)_2 \rightarrow 2H_2O + MgCl_2$

      b) 59.1 g, 1.014 mol,   **c)** 96.61 g, 1.014 mol.

121   **a)** $3MgCl_2 + Fe_2(SO_4)_3 \rightarrow 3MgSO_4 + 2FeCl_3$

      b) 62.9 g, 0.1574 mol,   **c)** 51.09 g, 0.3148 mol.

122   **a)** $4AgCl + Pb(OH)_4 \rightarrow 4AgOH + PbCl_4$

      b) 28.79 g, 0.1046 mol,   **c)** 36.53 g, 0.1046 mol.

123   **a)** $Zn(NO_3)_2 + 2KI \rightarrow ZnI_2 + 2KNO_3$

      b) 159.51 g, 0.9609 mol,   **c)** 97.15 g, 0.9609 mol.

124   **a)** $Cu(NO_3)_2 + Zn(OH)_2 \rightarrow Cu(OH)_2 + Zn(NO_3)_2$

      b) 10.6 g, 0.1067 mol,   **c)** 20.2 g, 0.1067 mol.

125   **a)** $Cr(OH)_3 + 3CuCl \rightarrow CrCl_3 + 3CuOH$

      b) 204.73 g, 2.068 mol,   **c)** 166.47 g, 2.068 mol.

126   **a)** $3FeO + 2AlF_3 \rightarrow 3FeF_2 + Al_2O_3$

      b) 64.74 g, 0.7707 mol,   **c)** 39.3 g, 0.3853 mol.

127   **a)** $H_2CO_3 + Ag_2O \rightarrow H_2O + Ag_2CO_3$

      b) 112.16 g, 0.4839 mol,   **c)** 133.45 g, 0.4839 mol.

128   **a)** $Li_2SO_4 + Cu(OH)_2 \rightarrow 2LiOH + CuSO_4$

      b) 64.82 g, 0.6648 mol,   **c)** 106.04 g, 0.6648 mol.

129   **a)** $Cu_2SO_4 + 2NaNO_3 \rightarrow 2CuNO_3 + Na_2SO_4$

      b) 49.55 g, 0.583 mol,   **c)** 41.39 g, 0.2915 mol.

130   **a)** $PbCl_4 + 2CdO \rightarrow PbO_2 + 2CdCl_2$

      b) 21.33 g, 0.1661 mol,   **c)** 30.46 g, 0.1661 mol.

131   **a)** $3ZnO + 2Al(NO_3)_3 \rightarrow 3Zn(NO_3)_2 + Al_2O_3$

      b) 115.14 g, 0.5405 mol,   **c)** 27.57 g, 0.2703 mol.

132   **a)** $6KOH + Al_2(CO_3)_3 \rightarrow 3K_2CO_3 + 2Al(OH)_3$

      b) 29.2 g, 0.1248 mol,   **c)** 19.47 g, 0.2496 mol.

133   **a)** $2LiCl + Mg(OH)_2 \rightarrow 2LiOH + MgCl_2$

      b) 30.94 g, 0.5307 mol,   **c)** 50.57 g, 0.5307 mol.

134   **a)** $3CaS + Fe_2O_3 \rightarrow 3CaO + Fe_2S_3$

      b) 73.79 g, 0.4623 mol,   **c)** 95.98 g, 0.4623 mol.

135   **a)** $CuO + ZnSO_4 \rightarrow CuSO_4 + ZnO$

      b) 140.08 g, 0.8679 mol,   **c)** 70.65 g, 0.8679 mol.

136   **a)** $3CuI + Al(OH)_3 \rightarrow 3CuOH + AlI_3$

      b) 7.65 g, 0.098 mol,   **c)** 39.97 g, 0.098 mol.

137   **a)** $CaSO_4 + 2HCl \rightarrow CaCl_2 + H_2SO_4$

      b) 38.08 g, 1.043 mol,   **c)** 51.12 g, 0.5217 mol.

138   **a)** $Cr_2(SO_4)_3 + 6AgCl \rightarrow 2CrCl_3 + 3Ag_2SO_4$

      b) 125.11 g, 0.8724 mol,   **c)** 136.01 g, 0.4362 mol.

139   **a)** $PbCl_4 + Cu_4P_2O_7 \rightarrow PbP_2O_7 + 4CuCl$

     b) 46.58 g, 0.1088 mol, **c)** 43.09 g, 0.4353 mol.

140   **a)** $3Mg(OH)_2 + Fe_2(CO_3)_3 \rightarrow 3MgCO_3 + 2Fe(OH)_3$

     b) 78.36 g, 0.2687 mol, **c)** 57.4 g, 0.5374 mol.

141   **a)** $2Al_2(CO_3)_3 + 3Pb(OH)_4 \rightarrow 4Al(OH)_3 + 3Pb(CO_3)_2$

     b) 38.81 g, 0.141 mol, **c)** 46.14 g, 0.141 mol.

142   **a)** $Na_2SO_4 + 2HBr \rightarrow 2NaBr + H_2SO_4$

     b) 75.2 g, 0.9296 mol, **c)** 45.55 g, 0.4648 mol.

143   **a)** $Cu_3(PO_4)_2 + 3Ag_2O \rightarrow 3CuO + 2Ag_3PO_4$

     b) 122.45 g, 0.5283 mol, **c)** 147.45 g, 0.3522 mol.

144   **a)** $2AgNO_3 + H_2CO_3 \rightarrow Ag_2CO_3 + 2HNO_3$

     b) 12.77 g, 0.206 mol, **c)** 25.96 g, 0.412 mol.

145   **a)** $CuO + Ca(ClO_2)_2 \rightarrow Cu(ClO_2)_2 + CaO$

     b) 110.13 g, 0.6289 mol, **c)** 35.28 g, 0.6289 mol.

146   **a)** $Pb(SO_4)_2 + 2ZnO \rightarrow PbO_2 + 2ZnSO_4$

     b) 19.58 g, 0.2405 mol, **c)** 38.81 g, 0.2405 mol.

147   **a)** $K_2SO_4 + 2HCl \rightarrow 2KCl + H_2SO_4$

     b) 26.82 g, 0.7348 mol, **c)** 36 g, 0.3674 mol.

148   **a)** $H_2SO_4 + 2KOH \rightarrow 2H_2O + K_2SO_4$

     b) 43.51 g, 0.7755 mol, **c)** 67.55 g, 0.3878 mol.

149   **a)** $H_2CO_3 + 2CuOH \rightarrow 2H_2O + Cu_2CO_3$

     b) 181.77 g, 2.258 mol, **c)** 211.13 g, 1.129 mol.

150   **a)** $2Al(OH)_3 + 3FeO \rightarrow Al_2O_3 + 3Fe(OH)_2$

     b) 132.55 g, 1.846 mol, **c)** 165.78 g, 1.846 mol.

151   **a)** $3HCl + Al(OH)_3 \rightarrow 3H_2O + AlCl_3$

     b) 66.96 g, 0.8584 mol, **c)** 114.6 g, 0.8584 mol.

152   **a)** $Cr_2S_3 + 3ZnO \rightarrow Cr_2O_3 + 3ZnS$

     b) 105.01 g, 1.29 mol, **c)** 125.65 g, 1.29 mol.

153   **a)** $K_2S + CuSO_4 \rightarrow K_2SO_4 + CuS$

     b) 121.58 g, 0.7623 mol, **c)** 72.79 g, 0.7623 mol.

154   **a)** $2LiOH + Cu(NO_3)_2 \rightarrow 2LiNO_3 + Cu(OH)_2$

     b) 164.75 g, 0.8787 mol, **c)** 85.67 g, 0.8787 mol.

155   **a)** $CdO + K_2SO_4 \rightarrow CdSO_4 + K_2O$

     b) 56.98 g, 0.3271 mol, **c)** 30.81 g, 0.3271 mol.

156   **a)** $2CuO + Pb(OH)_4 \rightarrow 2Cu(OH)_2 + PbO_2$

     b) 103.85 g, 0.3774 mol, **c)** 90.26 g, 0.3774 mol.

157   **a)** $Mg(ClO_2)_2 + CaCl_2 \rightarrow MgCl_2 + Ca(ClO_2)_2$

     b) 27.9 g, 0.2511 mol, **c)** 43.97 g, 0.2511 mol.

158   **a)** $Mg(OH)_2 + CaS \rightarrow MgS + Ca(OH)_2$

     b) 38.34 g, 0.5317 mol, **c)** 39.4 g, 0.5317 mol.

159   **a)** $FeCl_2 + Ag_2SO_4 \rightarrow FeSO_4 + 2AgCl$

     b) 209.01 g, 0.6703 mol, **c)** 192.26 g, 1.341 mol.

160   **a)** $3CuCl_2 + Cr_2(SO_4)_3 \rightarrow 3CuSO_4 + 2CrCl_3$

     b) 86.46 g, 0.2206 mol, **c)** 69.92 g, 0.4411 mol.

161   **a)** $2HCl + Ca(NO_3)_2 \rightarrow 2HNO_3 + CaCl_2$
      b) 132.63 g, 0.8082 mol, **c)** 89.79 g, 0.8082 mol.

162   **a)** $Cr(NO_3)_3 + 3CuCl \rightarrow CrCl_3 + 3CuNO_3$
      b) 61.15 g, 0.6176 mol, **c)** 77.51 g, 0.6176 mol.

163   **a)** $2KCl + Li_2CO_3 \rightarrow K_2CO_3 + 2LiCl$
      b) 40.07 g, 0.5429 mol, **c)** 46.04 g, 1.086 mol.

164   **a)** $2AlPO_4 + 3Ca(NO_3)_2 \rightarrow 2Al(NO_3)_3 + Ca_3(PO_4)_2$
      b) 42.37 g, 0.2582 mol, **c)** 26.71 g, 0.0861 mol.

165   **a)** $CuCO_3 + Li_2S \rightarrow CuS + Li_2CO_3$
      b) 27.81 g, 0.6073 mol, **c)** 44.82 g, 0.6073 mol.

166   **a)** $FeBr_2 + CuCO_3 \rightarrow FeCO_3 + CuBr_2$
      b) 54.42 g, 0.4406 mol, **c)** 98.39 g, 0.4406 mol.

167   **a)** $Fe(ClO)_2 + Ca(ClO_3)_2 \rightarrow Fe(ClO_3)_2 + Ca(ClO)_2$
      b) 61.3 g, 0.296 mol, **c)** 42.35 g, 0.296 mol.

168   **a)** $2LiNO_3 + K_2O \rightarrow Li_2O + 2KNO_3$
      b) 18.46 g, 0.1959 mol, **c)** 39.62 g, 0.3919 mol.

169   **a)** $Cr(OH)_3 + Al(NO_3)_3 \rightarrow Cr(NO_3)_3 + Al(OH)_3$
      b) 122.01 g, 0.5728 mol, **c)** 44.68 g, 0.5728 mol.

170   **a)** $CuCl_2 + Na_2S \rightarrow CuS + 2NaCl$
      b) 29.58 g, 0.3792 mol, **c)** 44.36 g, 0.7584 mol.

171   **a)** $3H_2SO_4 + Cr_2(CO_3)_3 \rightarrow 3H_2CO_3 + Cr_2(SO_4)_3$
      b) 76.31 g, 0.2687 mol, **c)** 105.33 g, 0.2687 mol.

172   **a)** $Mg(OH)_2 + Cu(ClO_2)_2 \rightarrow Mg(ClO_2)_2 + Cu(OH)_2$
      b) 122.57 g, 0.6175 mol, **c)** 60.21 g, 0.6175 mol.

173   **a)** $2Al_2O_3 + 3Zn_2P_2O_7 \rightarrow Al_4(P_2O_7)_3 + 6ZnO$
      b) 434.79 g, 1.426 mol, **c)** 232.23 g, 2.853 mol.

174   **a)** $CuCl_2 + H_2SO_4 \rightarrow CuSO_4 + 2HCl$
      b) 44.45 g, 0.4535 mol, **c)** 33.11 g, 0.9071 mol.

175   **a)** $3CuClO_2 + Al(OH)_3 \rightarrow 3CuOH + Al(ClO_2)_3$
      b) 17.27 g, 0.2214 mol, **c)** 50.81 g, 0.2214 mol.

176   **a)** $CuClO_2 + HNO_3 \rightarrow CuNO_3 + HClO_2$
      b) 46.17 g, 0.7328 mol, **c)** 50.2 g, 0.7328 mol.

177   **a)** $3Ca(OH)_2 + Cr_2(CO_3)_3 \rightarrow 3CaCO_3 + 2Cr(OH)_3$
      b) 68.99 g, 0.2429 mol, **c)** 50.04 g, 0.4858 mol.

178   **a)** $H_2S + 2AgOH \rightarrow 2H_2O + Ag_2S$
      b) 213.06 g, 1.706 mol, **c)** 211.36 g, 0.8529 mol.

179   **a)** $CuCO_3 + 2LiCl \rightarrow CuCl_2 + Li_2CO_3$
      b) 22.66 g, 0.5344 mol, **c)** 19.72 g, 0.2672 mol.

180   **a)** $Al(OH)_3 + Fe(NO_3)_3 \rightarrow Al(NO_3)_3 + Fe(OH)_3$
      b) 151.9 g, 0.6282 mol, **c)** 67.09 g, 0.6282 mol.

181   **a)** $2CuClO + Li_2CO_3 \rightarrow Cu_2CO_3 + 2LiClO$
      b) 25.03 g, 0.3391 mol, **c)** 39.61 g, 0.6783 mol.

182   **a)** $CaCO_3 + 2HNO_3 \rightarrow Ca(NO_3)_2 + H_2CO_3$
      b) 117.06 g, 1.858 mol, **c)** 57.6 g, 0.9291 mol.

183 a) $2HCl + Zn(OH)_2 \rightarrow 2H_2O + ZnCl_2$
b) 61.27 g, 0.6164 mol, c) 84.08 g, 0.6164 mol.

184 a) $PbO_2 + 2Cu(OH)_2 \rightarrow Pb(OH)_4 + 2CuO$
b) 48.91 g, 0.5017 mol, c) 39.88 g, 0.5017 mol.

185 a) $Pb_3(PO_4)_4 + 12LiOH \rightarrow 3Pb(OH)_4 + 4Li_3PO_4$
b) 26.34 g, 1.102 mol, c) 42.51 g, 0.3674 mol.

186 a) $3FeCl_2 + Al_2O_3 \rightarrow 3FeO + 2AlCl_3$
b) 10.19 g, 0.0999 mol, c) 26.67 g, 0.1998 mol.

187 a) $3Li_2O + Al_2S_3 \rightarrow 3Li_2S + Al_2O_3$
b) 82.21 g, 0.5481 mol, c) 55.91 g, 0.5481 mol.

188 a) $MgO + 2AgNO_3 \rightarrow Mg(NO_3)_2 + Ag_2O$
b) 193.93 g, 1.141 mol, c) 132.29 g, 0.5707 mol.

189 a) $2AgCl + H_2SO_4 \rightarrow Ag_2SO_4 + 2HCl$
b) 31.44 g, 0.3208 mol, c) 23.42 g, 0.6416 mol.

190 a) $Cr_2(SO_4)_3 + 6CuNO_3 \rightarrow 2Cr(NO_3)_3 + 3Cu_2SO_4$
b) 107.57 g, 0.8571 mol, c) 95.57 g, 0.4286 mol.

191 a) $3Fe(NO_3)_2 + Cr_2O_3 \rightarrow 3FeO + 2Cr(NO_3)_3$
b) 16.34 g, 0.1075 mol, c) 51.18 g, 0.2151 mol.

192 a) $3K_2SO_4 + 2Fe(ClO_2)_3 \rightarrow 6KClO_2 + Fe_2(SO_4)_3$
b) 43.49 g, 0.1684 mol, c) 33.64 g, 0.0842 mol.

193 a) $4LiCl + Pb(SO_4)_2 \rightarrow 2Li_2SO_4 + PbCl_4$
b) 58.84 g, 0.1474 mol, c) 51.47 g, 0.1474 mol.

194 a) $Cu(ClO)_2 + 2HCl \rightarrow CuCl_2 + 2HClO$
b) 12.71 g, 0.3483 mol, c) 18.29 g, 0.3483 mol.

195 a) $Cr(OH)_3 + 3CuNO_3 \rightarrow Cr(NO_3)_3 + 3CuOH$
b) 113.32 g, 0.9029 mol, c) 72.68 g, 0.9029 mol.

196 a) $CaO + ZnSO_4 \rightarrow CaSO_4 + ZnO$
b) 221.53 g, 1.373 mol, c) 111.73 g, 1.373 mol.

197 a) $HClO_2 + LiCl \rightarrow HCl + LiClO_2$
b) 43.95 g, 1.036 mol, c) 77.12 g, 1.036 mol.

198 a) $2AgCl + ZnSO_4 \rightarrow Ag_2SO_4 + ZnCl_2$
b) 41.08 g, 0.2545 mol, c) 34.72 g, 0.2545 mol.

199 a) 67 %, b) 0.3866 g.

200 a) 42 %, b) 1491 g.

201 a) 149.8 g, b) 8.322 mol.

202 a) 24.58 L, b) 5.616 g.

203 a) 83 %, b) 49.53 g.

204 a) 43.21 g, b) 2.4 mol.

205 a) 78.96 L, b) 16.81 g.

206 a) 268.4 g, b) 3.3 mol.

207 a) 81 %, b) 0.248 g.

208 a) 271.6 g, b) 2.111 mol.

209 a) 52 %.

210 a) 45 %, b) 9.18 g.

211	**a)** 144.6 g, **b)** 4.017 mol.
212	**a)** 67 %.
213	**a)** 61 %, **b)** 425.7 g.
214	**a)** 54 %, **b)** 101.1 g.
215	**a)** 3.285 L, **b)** 11.6 g.
216	**a)** 2.367 g, **b)** 0.06575 mol.
217	**a)** 691.9 g, **b)** 5.376 mol.
218	**a)** 82 %, **b)** 66.91 g.
219	**a)** 61 %.
220	**a)** 56 %, **b)** 355.5 g.
221	**a)** 81 %, **b)** 64.88 g.
222	**a)** 40 %, **b)** 17.4 g.
223	**a)** 332.6 g, **b)** 4.089 mol.
224	**a)** 36 %, **b)** 7.344 g.
225	**a)** 500.6 g, **b)** 3.102 mol.
226	**a)** 0.4117 L, **b)** 9.41 g.
227	**a)** 497.4 L, **b)** 828.2 g.
228	**a)** 60.84 g, **b)** 3.579 mol.
229	**a)** 37 %, **b)** 57.23 g.
230	**a)** 34 %.
231	**a)** 46 %, **b)** 0.6759 g.
232	**a)** 12.21 L, **b)** 70.65 g.
233	**a)** 56.41 g, **b)** 0.558 mol.
234	**a)** 78 %, **b)** 5.928 g.
235	**a)** 84 %, **b)** 366.1 g.
236	**a)** 23.19 g, **b)** 0.2293 mol.
237	**a)** 33 %, **b)** 1250 g.
238	**a)** 62.5 g, **b)** 3.472 mol.
239	**a)** 37.62 L, **b)** 30.21 g.
240	**a)** 22 L, **b)** 62.39 g.
241	**a)** 68 %, **b)** 342.1 g.
242	**a)** 10.41 L, **b)** 7.658 g.
243	**a)** 37 %, **b)** 3.182 g.
244	**a)** 64 %.
245	**a)** 35 %, **b)** 64.93 g.
246	**a)** 0.6595 g, **b)** 0.03664 mol.
247	**a)** 58 %, **b)** 90.48 g.
248	**a)** 50 %, **b)** 0.2449 g.
249	**a)** 66 %.
250	**a)** 64 %, **b)** 3.712 g.
251	**a)** 258.5 L, **b)** 52.65 g.
252	**a)** 51.3 g, **b)** 2.85 mol.
253	**a)** 200.1 L, **b)** 151.8 g.

254	**a)** 78 %.	
255	**a)** 46 %,	**b)** 2.484 g.
256	**a)** 38 %,	**b)** 43.48 g.
257	**a)** 30.46 g,	**b)** 1.792 mol.
258	**a)** 67 %,	**b)** 118.5 g.
259	**a)** 2.915 L,	**b)** 4.962 g.
260	**a)** 6.05 L,	**b)** 274.6 g.
261	**a)** 157.5 L,	**b)** 56.18 g.
262	**a)** 156.5 g,	**b)** 2.204 mol.
263	**a)** 59 %,	**b)** 217 g.
264	**a)** 16.85 g,	**b)** 0.936 mol.
265	**a)** 46 %.	
266	**a)** 40.12 L,	**b)** 27.88 g.
267	**a)** 53 %,	**b)** 1.802 g.
268	**a)** 46 %.	
269	**a)** 53 %,	**b)** 350.9 g.
270	**a)** 22.55 g,	**b)** 0.9395 mol.
271	**a)** 33 %,	**b)** 0.33 g.
272	**a)** 12.76 g,	**b)** 0.0967 mol.
273	**a)** 47 %.	
274	**a)** 63.78 L,	**b)** 46.93 g.
275	**a)** 1.321 L,	**b)** 19.08 g.
276	**a)** 24.16 L,	**b)** 24.41 g.
277	**a)** 42 %,	**b)** 489.8 g.
278	**a)** 174 g,	**b)** 9.666 mol.
279	**a)** 83.8 g,	**b)** 4.656 mol.
280	**a)** 1.994 g,	**b)** 0.1108 mol.
281	**a)** 13.46 g,	**b)** 0.792 mol.
282	**a)** 54 %,	**b)** 168.7 g.
283	**a)** 101.7 g,	**b)** 2.825 mol.
284	**a)** 721.3 g,	**b)** 40.07 mol.
285	**a)** 47 %,	**b)** 6.204 g.
286	**a)** 119.3 g,	**b)** 7.02 mol.
287	**a)** 42 %,	**b)** 73.92 g.
288	**a)** 73 %,	**b)** 53.95 g.
289	**a)** 174.3 L,	**b)** 205.9 g.
290	**a)** 53 %,	**b)** 3.869 g.
291	**a)** 53 %,	**b)** 21.88 g.
292	**a)** 50 %,	**b)** 237.7 g.
293	**a)** 84 %,	**b)** 178.7 g.
294	**a)** 339.4 g,	**b)** 19.96 mol.
295	**a)** 36.83 L,	**b)** 213.7 g.
296	**a)** 46 %,	**b)** 22.08 g.
297	**a)** 62.59 g,	**b)** 1.17 mol.

298   **a)** Al, aluminum,   **b)** 414.5 g.

299   **a)** H_2, hydrogen,   **b)** 133.4 g.

300   **a)** $Al(OH)_3$, aluminum hydroxide,   **b)** 31.41 g.

301   **a)** $Ca(OH)_2$, calcium hydroxide,   **b)** 235.7 g.

302   **a)** N_2, nitrogen,   **b)** 14.57 g.

303   **a)** H_2, hydrogen,   **b)** 34.86 g.

304   **a)** Zn, zinc,   **b)** 675.1 g.

305   **a)** HCl, hydrochloric acid,   **b)** 20.22 g.

306   **a)** NaOH, sodium hydroxide,   **b)** 19.84 g.

307   **a)** N_2, nitrogen,   **b)** 153.2 g.

308   **a)** NH_3, ammonia,   **b)** 32.33 g.

309   **a)** LiOH, lithium hydroxide,   **b)** 9.586 g.

310   **a)** HCl, hydrogen chloride,   **b)** 1400 g.

311   **a)** O_2, oxygen,   **b)** 79.85 g.

312   **a)** HCl, hydrochloric acid,   **b)** 371.8 g.

313   **a)** HCl, hydrochloric acid,   **b)** 63.4 g.

314   **a)** NaOH, sodium hydroxide,   **b)** 12.49 g.

315   **a)** H_2, hydrogen,   **b)** 50.61 g.

316   **a)** HCl, hydrochloric acid,   **b)** 71.82 g.

317   **a)** $Al(OH)_3$, aluminum hydroxide,   **b)** 38.39 g.

318   **a)** NH_3, ammonia,   **b)** 141.6 g.

319   **a)** N_2, nitrogen,   **b)** 262.8 g.

320   **a)** $HClO_3$, chloric acid,   **b)** 41.72 g.

321   **a)** H_2, hydrogen,   **b)** 100.1 g.

322   **a)** H_2SO_4, sulfuric acid,   **b)** 572.4 g.

323   **a)** H_2, hydrogen,   **b)** 40.89 g.

324   **a)** NaOH, sodium hydroxide,   **b)** 649.1 g.

325   **a)** CH_4, methane,   **b)** 4.319 g.

326   **a)** H_2, hydrogen,   **b)** 70.08 g.

327   **a)** N_2, nitrogen,   **b)** 92.33 g.

328   **a)** H_2SO_4, sulfuric acid,   **b)** 66.31 g.

329   **a)** $Ca(OH)_2$, calcium hydroxide,   **b)** 9.37 g.

330   **a)** H_2, hydrogen,   **b)** 25.65 g.

331   **a)** N_2, nitrogen,   **b)** 9.102 g.

332   **a)** HCl, hydrochloric acid,   **b)** 0.4932 g.

333   **a)** $Ca(OH)_2$, calcium hydroxide,   **b)** 12.16 g.

334   **a)** HCl, hydrochloric acid,   **b)** 9.863 g.

335   **a)** CO_2, carbon dioxide,   **b)** 71.15 g.

336   **a)** $Ca(OH)_2$, calcium hydroxide,   **b)** 50.18 g.

337   **a)** $Al(OH)_3$, aluminum hydroxide,   **b)** 48.77 g.

338   **a)** O_2, oxygen,   **b)** 57.86 g.

339   **a)** H_2, hydrogen,   **b)** 178.9 g.

340   **a)** CO_2, carbon dioxide,   **b)** 525 g.

341 **a)** NaOH, sodium hydroxide, **b)** 9.37 g.

342 **a)** HCl, hydrogen chloride, **b)** 69.24 g.

343 **a)** H_2, hydrogen, **b)** 268.3 g.

344 **a)** H_2SO_4, sulfuric acid, **b)** 29.63 g.

345 **a)** HCl, hydrochloric acid, **b)** 38.11 g.

346 **a)** $HClO_3$, chloric acid, **b)** 10.01 g.

347 **a)** O_2, oxygen, **b)** 590.3 g.

348 **a)** HCl, hydrochloric acid, **b)** 6.411 g.

349 **a)** LiOH, lithium hydroxide, **b)** 73.49 g.

350 **a)** $Al(OH)_3$, aluminum hydroxide, **b)** 59.74 g.

351 **a)** H_2SO_4, sulfuric acid, **b)** 15.43 g.

352 **a)** O_2, oxygen, **b)** 414.4 g.

353 **a)** NH_3, ammonia, **b)** 55.7 g.

354 **a)** O_2, oxygen, **b)** 66 g.

355 **a)** O_2, oxygen, **b)** 1117 g.

356 **a)** Zn, zinc, **b)** 53.19 g.

357 **a)** H_2, hydrogen, **b)** 17.4 g.

358 **a)** O_2, oxygen, **b)** 182.4 g.

359 **a)** O_2, oxygen, **b)** 95.99 g.

360 **a)** H_2SO_4, sulfuric acid, **b)** 5.51 g.

361 **a)** LiOH, lithium hydroxide, **b)** 6.178 g.

362 **a)** HCl, hydrochloric acid, **b)** 59.3 g.

363 **a)** H_2, hydrogen, **b)** 223.6 g.

364 **a)** NaOH, sodium hydroxide, **b)** 735 g.

365 **a)** KOH, potassium hydroxide, **b)** 93.08 g.

366 **a)** $Ca(OH)_2$, calcium hydroxide, **b)** 22.19 g.

367 **a)** H_2, hydrogen, **b)** 79.21 g.

368 **a)** $HClO_3$, chloric acid, **b)** 52.42 g.

369 **a)** $Al(OH)_3$, aluminum hydroxide, **b)** 244.3 g.

370 **a)** NH_3, ammonia, **b)** 944.1 g.

371 **a)** O_2, oxygen, **b)** 18.26 g.

372 **a)** Al, aluminum, **b)** 8.061 g.

373 **a)** $Ca(OH)_2$, calcium hydroxide, **b)** 63.86 g.

374 **a)** NH_3, ammonia, **b)** 64.49 g.

375 **a)** C_2H_4, ethene, **b)** 290.9 g.

376 **a)** HCl, hydrochloric acid, **b)** 336.6 g.

377 **a)** HCl, hydrochloric acid, **b)** 65.96 g.

378 **a)** Zn, zinc, **b)** 87.8 g.

379 **a)** H_2, hydrogen, **b)** 3.799 g.

380 **a)** Al, aluminum, **b)** 34.86 g.

381 **a)** HCl, hydrochloric acid, **b)** 83.55 g.

382 **a)** Zn, zinc, **b)** 1.233 g.

383 **a)** CO_2, carbon dioxide, **b)** 198.8 g.

384   **a)** HCl, hydrochloric acid,   **b)** 43.89 g.

385   **a)** HCl, hydrochloric acid,   **b)** 207.1 g.

386   **a)** $Al(OH)_3$, aluminum hydroxide,   **b)** 11.34 g.

387   **a)** H_2, hydrogen,   **b)** 102.5 g.

388   **a)** NaOH, sodium hydroxide,   **b)** 82.59 g.

389   **a)** $Al(OH)_3$, aluminum hydroxide,   **b)** 12.49 g.

390   **a)** HCl, hydrochloric acid,   **b)** 41.67 g.

391   **a)** O_2, oxygen,   **b)** 72.54 g.

392   **a)** $Ca(OH)_2$, calcium hydroxide,   **b)** 88.19 g.

393   **a)** NaOH, sodium hydroxide,   **b)** 6.904 g.

394   **a)** O_2, oxygen,   **b)** 70.36 g.

395   **a)** O_2, oxygen,   **b)** 6044 g.

396   **a)** Al, aluminum,   **b)** 0.3061 g.

Printed in Great Britain
by Amazon